THE CESSNA 172
A PILOTS GUIDE

JEREMY M. PRATT

First Edition 1993

Copyright © 1993 Airplan Flight Equipment & JEREMY M. PRATT

THE CESSNA 172 A PILOTS GUIDE
JEREMY M. PRATT

ISBN: 1 874783 35 7

Airplan Flight Equipment, Southside, Manchester International Airport,
Wilmslow, Cheshire SK9 4LL, U.K. Tel: 061-499 0023   Fax: 061-499 0298

Acknowledgments

I would like to thank all those whose knowledge, help and advice went into this book, in particular :

Farooq Ahmed

CAA Safety Promotion Section

Colourmatch

Cheshire Air Training School

Deltair

Adrian Dickinson

Steve Dickinson

George Firbank

East Midlands Flying School

Peggy Follis

David Hockings

Andy Holland

Light Planes (Lancs) Ltd

Luton Flight Training

Manchester School of Flying

Steve Maffitt

Chris Nolan

Andy Parker

Ravenair

Neil Rigby

Ian Sixsmith

John Thorpe

Visual Eyes

Sarah, Kate and Miles

Jeremy M Pratt
June 1993

Contents

Section 1 - General Description

Section 2 - Limitations

Section 3 – Handling the Cessna 172

Section 4 – Mixture and Carb Icing Supplement

Section 5 – Expanded C 172 Pre-Flight Check List

© Airplan Flight Equipment 1993

Section 6 – Cessna 172 Loading and Performance

Section 7 – Conversions

THIS AFE PILOT GUIDE IS NOT AN AUTHORITATIVE DOCUMENT AND SHOULD NOT BE TAKEN AS SUCH

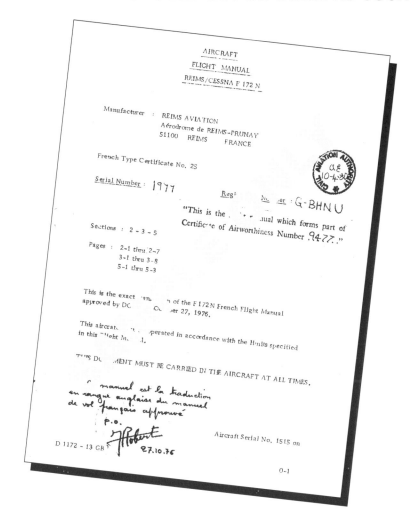

The approved Pilot Operating Handbook/Flight Manual (illustrated above), as amended, is the only source of authoritative information. Each individual aircraft has its own individual POH/FM, in the interests of safety & good airmanship the pilot should be familiar with this document.

The Cessna 172

The Cessna 172, in its many variants and spin offs' must be the leading contender for the title of the world's most popular light plane.

The production statistics alone are staggering; an overall production (depending on which models and types you choose to include) of around 42000 and a peak production rate of about one aircraft every 30 minutes, in a production run lasting from 1955 through to 1985. The 172 makes a natural progression for those trained on Cessna 150s or 152s, and has a well earned reputation for being safe and forgiving, with few airframe or engine problems.

This book covers the 172s built from 1977 through to 1985 (models 172N and 172P). These models are powered by the Lycoming 0-320 engine of 160Hp, replacing the 150Hp version, which itself had replaced the six cylinder continental engines in the 1960s. The 172 is popularly referred to as the 'Skyhawk/100' and the 'Skyhawk/100 II' which was sold with an increased standard package including an avionics fit. As with other Cessna models a significant number were manufactured by Reims Aviation in France. These models are identical to American built examples, but carry the 'F' prefix to their model number.

The 172N is powered by the 0-320-H2AD engine which proved to be an expensive proposition, contrary to previous 172 powerplants. It was subject to various AD's (Airworthiness Directives), oil additives and special operating procedures as a result of problems in the valve train. The controversial situation with the H2AD engine continued until 1981 when a new model of engine - the D2J - was introduced, which appears to have been altogether better. Also in this year the maximum flap extension was reduced from 40° to 30° and the gross weight was increased by 100lbs. In addition the landing and taxy lights were moved from the lower cowling to the leading edge of the port wing. This final version of the Skyhawk is designated the 172P.

Production of the 172 ended in 1985, another victim of the problems affecting the General Aviation industry in the early 1980s. It is doubtful that any other aircraft will surpass the 172 for production and popularity, and it is certain to have the same longevity as its 150 and 152 stable mates.

Model Numbers and Production Years

PRODUCTION YEAR	MODEL	MODEL NAME
1977 - 1980	172 N	Skyhawk/Skyhawk II
1977 - 1980	F172 N	Reims/Cessna F 172 Skyhawk/Skyhawk II
1981 - 1986	172 P	Skyhawk/Skyhawk II
1981 - 1986	F172 P	F 172 Skyhawk/Skyhawk II

The Cessna 172

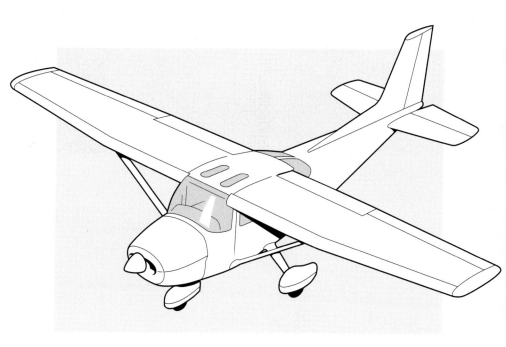

General Description

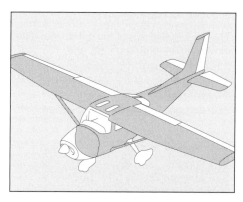

The Airframe

The Cessna 172 airframe can be described as being of all metal construction, the primary structure being constructed of aluminium alloy. Some non-structural components such as the wing tips and wing strut fairings are made from GRP.

The fuselage has a semi-monocoque structure, that is the vertical bulkheads and frames are joined by horizontal longerons and stringers which run the length of the fuselage. The metal skin is rivetted to this structure, this arrangement is conventional for modern light aircraft and allows loads to be spread over the whole construction. At the rear of the fuselage the tail unit consists of a swept fin with rudder and conventional tailplane with elevators. Underneath the rear fuselage a metal loop tie down point and tail guard is fitted. This loop is vulnerable to damage in a 'tail-strike'. It is possible for this loop to be pushed back into the base of the rudder. Small holes are drilled in the underneath of the fuselage to act as drainage points. If it is suspected that water has entered the rear fuselage, the tail should be lowered and any water should drain from these holes (as long as they aren't blocked of course).

The wings are of semi-cantilever design (supported by an external strut) and have a 1° dihedral. Where each strut meets the underwing a metal ring is fitted to be used as a tie down point.

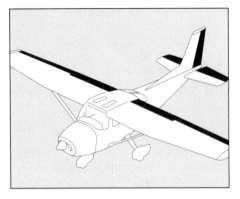

The Flying Controls

Dual flight controls are fitted as standard and link the cockpit controls to the control surfaces via cable linkages.

The AILERONS are of the differential type, moving upward through 20° and downward through 15°. Balance weights are incorporated at the lower inner edge of the ailerons, the aileron design also incorporates a degree of Frise action.

The FLAPS are slotted, and incorporate a degree of Fowler action over the first 10°. The flaps are electrically operated, and can be set between 0° and 40° (172N) and from 0° and 30° (172P). The flaps are electrically operated via a pre-selectable switch to the right of the mixture control. To select a flap setting the lever is moved to the desired setting - the control is gated in 10° stages - and a small indicator next to the lever will show the actual flap movement. This arrangement is very simple to use and a vast improvement on the original system where the lever had to be held down whilst the flaps travelled to the desired position.

The 'gated' flap switch of the 172N

The cockpit control lock fixes the elevators and ailerons. When properly fitted the label should cover the master switch and magneto switch.

The RUDDER is operated from the rudder pedals (which are also linked to the steerable nose wheel) and can move through 16° either side of the neutral position.

On the trailing edge of the control surface a ground adjustable trim tab is fitted, a horn balance is incorporated in the upper forward portion of the control surface (ahead of the hinge line).

Late model 172s have a spring loaded rudder trim control, operated by a lever under the elevator trim control.

The ELEVATORS are fitted to the tailplane, and move up through 28° and down through 23°. They incorporate a horn balance at their outer forward edge ahead of the hinge line.

A ground adjustable trim tab is fitted to the trailing edge of the rudder.

Cockpit rudder trim control.

An adjustable TRIM TAB is fitted to the right hand elevator. Operation of the cockpit trim wheel (located below the throttle) moves this control surface independently of the elevator control. On the 172N the trim tab moves through 28° up and 13° down. On the 172P with the reduced full flap deflection the trim tab movement is 22° up and 19° down. An indicator mounted next to the cockpit trim wheel shows the trim position set, and the control works in the natural sense, ie trimming the wheel forward gives nose down trim and vice versa.

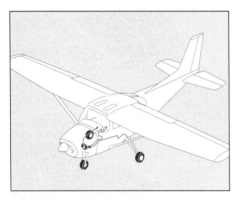

The Undercarriage

The 172 undercarriage is fixed and of the tricycle type. The main gear is a tubular steel undercarriage leg, surrounded by a full length fairing and fitted with a step. The main gear attaches to the lower fuselage, with a plastic fairing where the leg joins the lower fuselage.

The main gear has an 8' 4" track - the distance between the two main wheels.

The nose gear attaches to the engine mount and has an air/oil oleo strut to damp and absorb the normal operating loads. On the rear of the nose leg a torque link is fitted to maintain the correct alignment of the nose wheel, its lower arm is fitted to the nose wheel fork and the upper arm to the oleo cylinder casing. Also fitted to the nose leg is a small cylinder-piston unit, the shimmy damper. The purpose of this unit is to reduce nose wheel shimmy (rapid oscillation of the nose wheel, felt as vibration through the rudder pedals) which is most prevalent during take off and landing.

The nose gear is steerable through a spring linkage to the rudder pedals. The rudder pedals turn the nosewheel through 10° either side of neutral. The use of differential braking allows the nosewheel to castor up to 30°.

Main gear unit

The braking system consists of single disc brake assemblies fitted to the main undercarriage and operated by a hydraulic system. The brakes are operated through the upper portion of each rudder pedal. The pilot's (left hand side) toe brakes have a separate brake cylinder above each pedal, and it is possible to operate the brakes differentially - to the port or starboard wheel. Where co-pilot (right) side pedals are also fitted with toe brakes they are mechanically linked to the pilot side brake cylinders. The system of toe brakes allows the aircraft to turn in a very tight circle, and it is possible to lock one main wheel with the use of some toe brake force. Turning around a wheel in this fashion tends to 'scrub' the tyre and can also cause excessive forces on the tyre side wall, it is generally discouraged.

The parking brake set to 'ON'.   *The parking brake 'OFF'.*

A parking brake is located in front of the left hand seat. With the parking brake OFF, the handle is horizontal against the lower instrument panel. To operate the parking brake the handle is pulled out (a distinct pressure will be felt) and then turned 1/4 turn down , the lever should remain in this position to show that the parking brake is ON. Unfortunately it is quite easy to knock this lever accidentally, in which case it may well spring back to the OFF position, so care should be taken to ensure that the parking brake is properly engaged when required.

The main wheels are fitted with 600 X 6 tyres as standard, the nose wheel with 500 X 5. The tyre grooves should have not less than 2mm depth over 75% of the tyre to be serviceable. If the tread across the width of the tyre is worn to less than 2mm in any one place the tyre will need replacing.

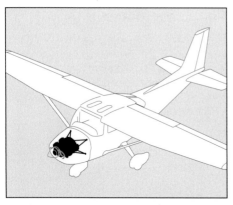

The Engine

The 172 N is fitted with a Lycoming O-320-H2AD engine, the 172 P is fitted with an O-320-D2J, both versions are rated at 160 HP at 2700 RPM.

The engine is a four cylinder unit, with cylinders horizontally opposed across the crankshaft. The cylinders are staggered so that each connecting rod has its own crankshaft throw, the cylinders and crankcase assembly are fashioned from aluminium alloy castings.

The engine is air cooled. Airflow enters the engine compartment at the front of the cowling, and is directed by baffles to flow over the whole engine. The cylinders feature deep fins to aid cooling, the airflow leaves the engine compartment at the lower cowling underneath the engine compartment.

The engine is mounted on a steel tubular mounting which attaches to the firewall. From here fuselage stringers attach to the forward door posts.

The 0-320-H2AD engine used in the 172 N has been subject to several Airworthiness Directives (ADs) and service bulletins as a result of problems with the valve train. Although these are largely of concern to the engineers it should be noted that special oil additives may be required for the 172 N.

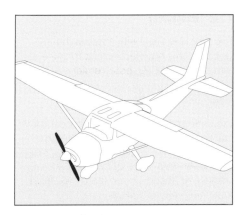

The Propeller

The propeller is an all metal, two bladed, fixed pitch design, turned by direct drive from the engine crankshaft, the propeller rotates clockwise as seen from the cockpit. The diameter is 75"/1.91m, with a minimum of 74"/1.88m.

The Cessna-172 propeller.

The Ignition System

The engine features a dual ignition system, fitted with two magnetos. The magnetos are small electrical AC generators which are driven by the crankshaft rotation to provide a very high voltage to a distributor, which directs it via high voltage leads (or high tension leads) to the spark plugs. At the spark plug the current must cross a gap, in doing so a spark is produced which ignites the fuel/air mixture in the cylinder.

The magnetos are fitted at the rear of the engine, one each side of the engine centre line (hence Left and Right magnetos). The usual arrangement is for each magneto to fire one of the two spark plugs in each cylinder, each cylinder has two spark plugs (top and bottom) for safety and efficiency. The leads that run from the magnetos to the spark plugs should be secure and there should be no splits or cracks in the plastic insulation covering the leads.

It is worth emphasising that the ignition system is totally independent of the aircraft electrical system, and once the engine is running it will operate regardless of the serviceability of the battery or alternator.

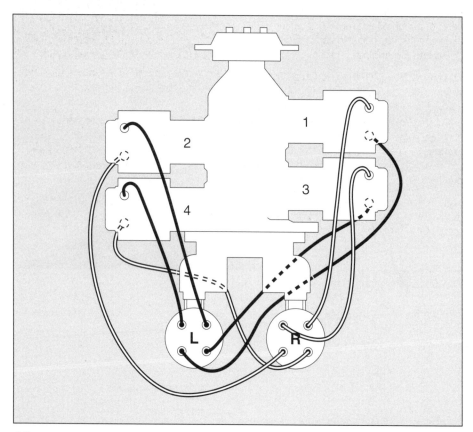

The Oil System

The oil system of the engine provides for lubrication, cooling, sealing, cleansing and protection against corrosion. The system is a wet sump, pressure feed system. The oil sump is located under the engine, and oil is drawn from there , through a filter by the engine driven oil pump and to a bypass valve. This valve routes the oil to the oil cooler when the oil is hot, from there the oil passes through a pressure relief valve, and then into the oil gallery of the crankcase. When the oil has flowed around the engine it drains down to the sump by gravity. The function of the pressure relief valve is to regulate the oil pressure over a wide range of temperatures and power settings. In the case of a high oil pressure the valve allows oil to return to the sump without going into the engine.

The oil filler pipe is accessible under the upper cowling inspection hatch.

Oil contents can be checked on a dipstick which is accessible from the upper cowling inspection hatch. The dipstick is graduated in US quarts and measures the contents of the oil sump. When the engine has been running, the oil may take up to 10 minutes to return to the sump, only then can a true reading be taken. When replacing the dipstick care should be taken not to overtighten the cap. To do so can make it exceptionally difficult to open the cap again, and it is quite possible to strip the thread on the cap or filler pipe.

The oil temperature gauge mounted in the cockpit is electrically operated and measures temperature from a sender unit in the engine. The oil pressure gauge gives a direct reading from a pressure pick up in the engine.

The Starter System

The starter motor is housed at the lower front left side of the engine. It incorporates a geared cog that engages on to the teeth of the starter ring when the key starter is operated. As the engine is turned an impulse coupling in the magneto operates, this retards the spark and aids starting. When the engine fires and begins to rotate under its own power this impulse coupling ceases to operate and normal spark timing is resumed. When the key starter is released, allowing it to return to the 'BOTH' position, the cog on the starter motor withdraws to be clear of the starter ring.

A STARTER WARNING LIGHT is fitted in the cockpit. This illuminates when the starter is operated to show that the starter motor is engaging the starter ring. When the key starter is released the light should go out. If the light remains on this means that the starter motor is still engaged to the starter ring. In this instance the starter motor is being turned by the engine, and serious damage may be caused to the aircraft electrical system. In this case the engine should be shut down without delay.

The starter warning light located close to the magneto switch.

The Fuel System

The 172 has two aluminium fuel tanks, located one in each wing and joined by a balance pipe. From each tank a fuel line runs down the inner fuselage and on to the fuel selector valve. From this valve the fuel line runs to a fuel strainer mounted on the firewall, and from there to the carburettor. A separate line runs from the strainer to the cockpit primer and from there to the cylinder intake ports. The fuel system is of the simple gravity feed type.

When checking fuel contents before flight it is VITAL to check fuel contents VISUALLY, the cockpit fuel gauges are not accurate enough to assess true fuel contents. When the fuel contents have been visually checked care must be taken to replace the fuel caps securely. If the caps are loose or cross-threaded fuel may vent out from the tank during flight.

During the pre-flight inspection a visual check of the fuel contents is essential. Many operators provide steps or a ladder for this purpose.

The high wing Cessna singles feature in accidents caused by fuel exhaustion. More often than not the fuel tanks were NOT visually checked during the pre-flight checks, and the fuel ran out even though the gauges were indicating that sufficient fuel remained. In some unexplained fuel exhaustion accidents loss of fuel due to a cross threaded fuel cap is suspected. Due to the balance pipe between the two fuel tanks, a loose cap on one tank may draw out the fuel from BOTH tanks. The high wing design of the 172 can lead to a reluctance by the pilot to climb up and visually check the contents. It is for this reason that the 172 is fitted with a step on each wing strut and a grab handle on each side of the upper cowling to aid access to the upper wing.

When refuelling, the fuel selector should be placed in the LEFT or RIGHT position to minimise cross feeding between tanks (especially if parked on a sloping surface).

In a gravity feed fuel system positive VENTING is of great importance. The left tank has a forward facing pipe on the lower inboard surface of the left wing to provide atmospheric pressure for venting. The pipe is located directly behind the wing strut to protect it from icing, and it ensures that ambient pressure is maintained above the fuel in the fuel tank. The right hand fuel cap is vented, although both fuel\caps may be vented on some aircraft. Should the vents become blocked a depression will form in the tank as the fuel level lowers, and fuel flow to the engine may be interrupted.

There are three FUEL STRAINERS, one at the lower rear inboard edge of each tank, accessible from the inboard lower wing surface, and one from the fuel strainer bowl. The tank strainers can be checked using a fuel tester equipped with a pin to take a fuel sample for inspection. The fuel bowl strainer is operated by a control located under the upper cowling inspection flap. When this control is operated (by pulling) fuel will run from a pipe in the region of the nose leg. To collect fuel from this pipe whilst operating the drainer can be very difficult, but fuel should not be allowed to merely run onto the ground, as water or contaminated fuel could go undetected. Fuel can only be drawn from the strainer bowl if the cockpit fuel selector is in the Left, Right or Both position. It is imperative to ensure that the fuel strainer control is pushed back in to the OFF position after use, or fuel may continue to drain from the pipe out of view of the pilot.

The cockpit FUEL SELECTOR is located on the floor under the instrument panel and easily accessible to each pilot. The selector can be used to feed the engine from either the Left or Right tank, or Both tanks simultaneously. To turn the fuel OFF the pointer is turned to face directly aft (behind). There is no safety guard on the OFF position, so care should be exercised when turning the pointer. For all normal operations the fuel selector should be placed in the BOTH position. It is possible for the tank levels to become uneven when the fuel selector is in the Both position, and so the Left or Right tank can be selected in cruising flight to keep the tank levels even. With a low fuel tank level (below approximately 1/4 full), prolonged uncoordinated manoeuvres such as sideslips or skidding flight should be avoided, as the fuel tank outlet may become uncovered and fuel supply will be interrupted. For the same reason extreme 'running' take offs are not recommended.

The cockpit fuel selector.
Here fuel is selected 'OFF'.

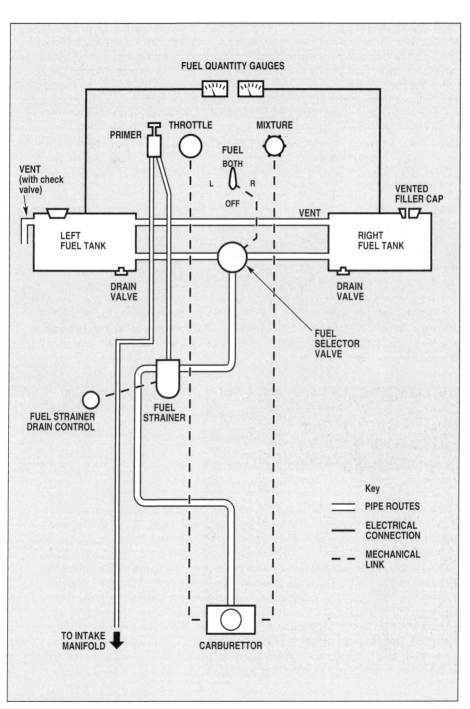

The Carburettor

The carburettor mixes air with the fuel from the fuel system and supplies the fuel/air mix to the cylinders. The carburettor is located under the engine, and takes induction air from a scoop intake in the lower front cowling. This air is filtered and then fed into the carburettor air box. In this box a butterfly valve is used to allow either the induction air, or heated air, to be fed to the carburettor. Heated air comes from an unfiltered inlet pipe which then passes into a shroud around the exhaust which heats it before it reaches the carburettor. Hot or cold air is selected via the carburettor heat control in the cockpit, the use of this control and the subject of carburettor icing are discussed fully later in this book. From the carburettor the fuel/air mix is carried to the induction manifold which feeds the fuel/air mix to the intake port of each cylinder.

The primer control, to the left of the magneto switch.

There is a manual fuel PRIMER system, which is an aid to starting, operated from a primer control mounted on the far left of the instrument panel. To unlock the primer it is rotated until the pin aligns with a cut out in the collar allowing the control to be pulled out. When the control is pulled out it draws fuel from the fuel strainer bowl, when pushed in the primer delivers fuel through the priming line to the intake port of the number 4 cylinder. As an option a three cylinder priming system may be fitted which delivers fuel to the number 1, 2 and 4 cylinders. A cold engine will typically require three cycles on the primer. To lock the primer the control is pushed in ensuring the pin is aligned with the cut out in the collar, the control should then be rotated through about half a turn. To check the primer is fully locked: attempt to pull the control out, this should not be possible. It is essential to make sure the primer is locked in the closed position, as if it is not engine rough running may well result.

The MIXTURE is controlled from the mixture control located on the lower instrument panel, which adjusts the fuel/air ratio in the carburettor. The vernier mixture control is moved by depressing a button in the centre of the control and moving the control In or Out. For fine adjustment the control can be rotated clockwise to enrich the mixture, and anti-clockwise to lean the mixture. In the fully forward position it gives a RICH mixture, and if pulled fully out to the ICO (Idle Cut Off) position the fuel supply is cut off and the engine will stop.

The THROTTLE is located to the left of the mixture control, it is also of a push/pull type, but does not have the vernier fine adjustment feature of the mixture control. The throttle does have a friction nut at the point where it joins the instrument panel, when this nut is rotated clockwise the throttle movement becomes more difficult, when rotated anti-clockwise the throttle movement becomes loose.

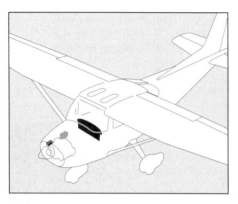

The Electrical System

Up to the 1978 models the 172 has a 14 volt, direct current electrical system. After 1978 models a 28 volt system is installed. A 60 amp alternator is mounted to the front lower right of the engine and is engine driven from a belt drive to a ring directly behind the starter ring. A 12 volt (pre 1978) or 24 volt (1978 and on) battery is located inside a vented box on the forward left side of the firewall.

The ALTERNATOR is the primary source of power to the electrical system in normal operations with the engine running. The alternator produces alternating current (AC) which is converted into direct current (DC) by diodes incorporated in the alternator housing which act as rectifiers. By their design alternators require a small voltage (about 3 volts) to produce the electromagnetic field required inside the alternator. The significance of this is that if the battery is completely discharged (flat), the alternator will not be able to supply any power to the electrical system, even after the engine has been started by some other means (ie external power or hand swinging). Output from the alternator is controlled by a VOLTAGE REGULATOR which is mounted on the left side of the firewall. An OVERVOLTAGE SENSOR protects the system from possible damage due to an overvoltage condition. In the event of a high voltage the relay opens and the alternator can be assumed to have failed.

The primary purpose of the BATTERY is to provide power for engine starting, the initial excitation of the alternator and as a backup in the event of alternator failure. In normal operations with the engine running the alternator provides the power to the electrical system and charges the battery. A fully charged battery has a charging current of about 2 amperes, in a partially discharged condition (ie just after engine start) the charging rate can be much higher than this. In the event of an alternator failure the battery is providing ALL power to the electrical system. The ampere rating of the battery will vary depending on the exact model and battery option installed. In theory a fully charged battery of say 15 ampere hours is capable of providing 15 amps for 1 hour, or 1 amp for 15 hours, or 7.5 amps for 2 hours etc. In practice the power available is governed by factors such as battery age and condition, load placed on it etc. The best advice is to reduce electrical load to the minimum consistent with safety, and plan to make a landing at the earliest opportunity.

The AMMETER is located on the instrument panel and indicates the current in amps to or from the battery. Should the alternator fail the ammeter will show a discharge, the flow out of the battery to the electrical system.

Up to 1978 aircraft a 'HIGH VOLTAGE' warning light is fitted. In the event of a high voltage condition occurring, the over-voltage sensor will shut down the alternator. The red high voltage warning light will then illuminate to show that the battery is supplying all electrical power. On 1979 models and after this light is replaced with a red 'LOW VOLTAGE' warning light.

The master switch is here set so that the battery is providing all the power to the electrical system, the alternator is 'off-line'. The 'Low voltage' light is illuminated and the ammeter is showing a discharge.

This light will illuminate at any time when the alternator has failed or been shut down, or when voltage has dropped below approx. 24 volts, and the battery is supplying all electrical power. On earlier aircraft this light may be fitted in addition to the high voltage warning light. During operations at low engine RPMs (ie during taxying) it is not unusual for the low voltage light to illuminate intermittently. However once higher RPMs are restored the light should go out.

The pilot controls the electrical system via the MASTER SWITCH located on the left side of the instrument panel. This switch is a split rocker switch having two halves, labelled 'BAT' and 'ALT', and normally the switch is operated as one, both halves being used together. The 'BAT' half of the switch can be operated independently, so that all electrical power is being drawn from the battery only; however the 'ALT' side can only be turned on in conjunction with the 'BAT' half, for the reasons covered previously. Should an electrical problem occur the MASTER Switch can be used to reset the electrical system by turning it OFF for 2 seconds and then turning it ON again.

The 172 has a split bus bar, one side providing power to the electrical accessories and the other supplying the avionics. The bus bar is essentially a conductor which distributes power to electrical services. From 1978 models a separate 'AVIONICS POWER SWITCH' may be fitted to control the avionics bus bar separately to the rest of the electrical system. This switch is normally OFF before engine starting to prevent avionics being damaged by transient high voltages during the engine start.

The aircraft may be fitted with an EXTERNAL POWER RECEPTACLE as an option. This can be used to connect external power for starting or operation of the aircraft electrical system. The receptacle is located under a door in the left side engine cowling.Before using external power it is imperative to check that the external power unit is of the correct voltage - otherwise SERIOUS DAMAGE COULD BE INFLICTED ON THE ELECTRICAL SYSTEM. Additionally it should be remembered that if the battery is totally flat (completely discharged), it will need to be removed and recharged or replaced before flight. When using external power the avionics master switch (if fitted) should be turned off when the external power source is being connected, although the main master switch should be ON.

The various electrically operated systems are protected by individual CIRCUIT BREAKERS, which are located in a line along the lower edge of the instrument panel. Should a problem (ie a short circuit) occur the relevant circuit breaker may 'pop', and will be seen to be raised in relation to the other circuit breakers (CBs). The correct procedure is to allow the CB to cool for say 2 minutes, then reset it and check the result. If the CB pops again it should not be reset. All CBs show their rating and the components they protect.

Apart from engine starting and alternator field the electrical system supplies power to the following:

ALL internal and external lights.
ALL radios and intercom.
Wing flaps, Pitot heater.
Turn coordinator.
Fuel gauges, Oil temperature gauge.

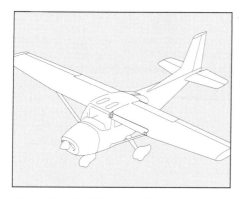

The Stall Warner System

A reed switch connected to an intake in the left wing leading edge gives an aural stall warning via a horn situated behind the upper left hand door post cover in the cockpit. When the stalling angle of attack is approached the airflow over the leading edge causes a suction through the reed producing a loud tone, which becomes increasingly high pitched as the stalling angle of attack is reached. Typically the stall warner activates 5 - 10 Kts above the stall speed.

The stall warner intake in the left wing leading edge.

To check the function of the stall warner on the ground the intake should be checked for blockages, and a suction can be applied by sucking air through the intake. If this is done it is recommended that a handkerchief or something similar be placed over the intake first, to avoid the unpleasant possibility of swallowing any insects stuck in the intake.

The Lighting System

The 172 may be equipped with a variety of optional internal and external lighting. When wing tip 'strobe' lights are fitted care should be taken in their use. As a general rule strobes are not used during taxying as they can dazzle and distract those nearby, they are however very effective in the air. If flying in cloud conditions or heavy precipitation it is recommended that they be turned off as the pilot may become spatially disoriented. The landing light is fitted in the lower front nose cowling up to 1982 models, lights of increased power are fitted in the left wing leading edge in models after this date. The landing and taxy lights should be used with some discretion, not least because of the very short life of the lamp bulbs. Other external lights are controlled from rocker switches in the line along the lower left side instrument panel.

The internal panel and radio lights are controlled from a rheostat type circular control located under the throttle. Turning the inner knob adjusts the brightness of the radio lights, and the outer rim adjusts the panel lights.

There may be a slide switch on the overhead console which enables flood lighting or door post lighting (or both together) to be selected. Another option is a map light in the left door post or in the left control wheel. There is also an overhead 'dome' light located in the cabin ceiling, this light is of a set brightness and has an on/off switch located on its side. Given the wide variety of options available it is best to check the system on the individual aircraft you intend to fly, especially before night flying.

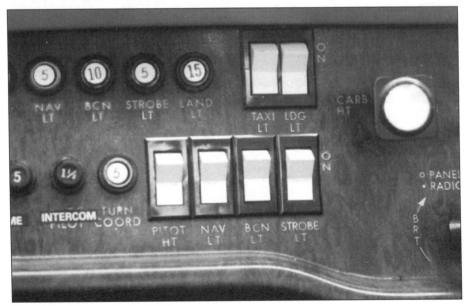

The light switches of a C-172N

© Airplan Flight Equipment 1993

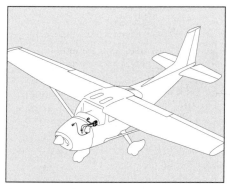

The Vacuum System

An engine driven vacuum pump is mounted to the upper rear face of the engine. This pump is fitted with a plastic shear drive, so that should the pump seize, the drive will shear and the engine will not be damaged. The air enters the suction system through a filter mounted below the instrument panel, passes through the air driven gyro instruments (and is measured for the suction gauge), flows through a vacuum regulator and into the vacuum pump, from which it is expelled through a short pipe.

Suction is used to drive the gyros in the Attitude Indicator (or Artificial Horizon) and Heading Indicator (or Direction Indicator). A gauge mounted on the instrument panel measures suction, for cruising RPMs and altitudes the reading should be between 4.5 and 5.4 inches of mercury, at higher or lower suction the gyros may become unreliable. A lower suction over an extended period may indicate a faulty vacuum regulator, dirty screens or a system leak. If the vacuum pump fails or a line collapses the suction gauge reading will fall to zero, and the Attitude Indicator and Heading Indicator will

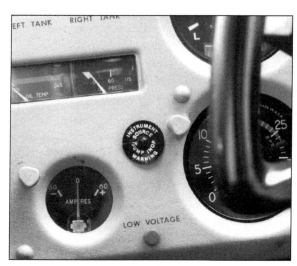

become unreliable over a period of some minutes as the gyros run down losing RPM. The real danger here is that the effect is gradual and may not be noticed by the pilot for some time.

Late model 172s may be fitted with a red 'LOW VACUUM' warning light, which alerts the pilot to check the suction gauge for a possible vacuum system fault.

The low vacuum warning light.

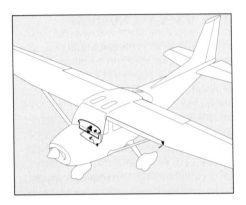

The Pitot-Static System

The pitot-static system provides static pressure to the Vertical Speed Indicator (VSI) and Altimeter and pitot and static pressure to the Airspeed Indicator (ASI).

The pitot head under the left wing.

Pitot pressure comes from a PITOT HEAD which is located under the left wing. Static pressure comes from a STATIC VENT located on the forward left fuselage ahead of the left cabin door.

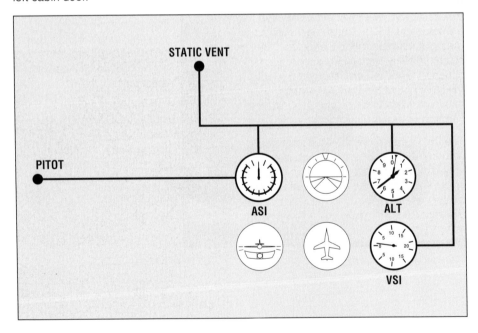

© Airplan Flight Equipment 1993

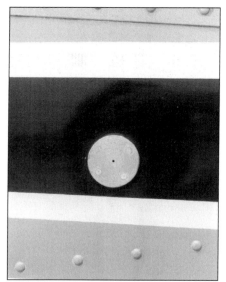

The static vent on the left fuselage ahead of the door.

No checking system is incorporated in the system, and instrument indications in the event of a leak or blockage are outside of the scope of this book. As an option the pitot head has a heating element which is activated by a switch in the electrical rocker switch group in front of the pilot. Pitot heat can prevent blockage of the pitot head in heavy rain or icing, this notwithstanding it must be remembered that the 172 IS NOT CLEARED FOR FLIGHT INTO KNOWN ICING CONDITIONS. An alternate static source may be fitted in the cockpit in case of suspected blockage of the external static vent. The control is pulled out to select the alternate static source from inside the cockpit, when in use the pressure instruments will have errors, dependent on the use of cabin heaters, fresh air vents and windows. These errors will be somewhere in the region of 5 knots in airspeed and 30 feet in altitude, however the aircraft flight manual may have a table giving more precise figures for the particular circumstances. Where an alternate static source is NOT fitted, static pressure can be fed to the altimeter and ASI by smashing the instrument face of the VSI, thus allowing static pressure from the cabin to enter the static system. This action is fairly extreme (and expensive) and will probably require using the blunt end of the fire extinguisher, therefore it should be reserved for use in a genuine emergency.

The external static vent should be checked before flight to ensure that it is clear and unobstructed. A similar check is carried out on the pitot head, which may be protected on the ground with a removable pitot cover. It is important not to blow into either pitot or static vent, doing so can result in damage to the pressure instruments.

The optional 'Alternate static air' which senses static pressure in the cockpit.

The Heating and Ventilation System

Cabin heating is supplied via a muffler shroud around the engine exhaust system. This allows air to be warmed by the exhaust pipes, it is then directed to outlets in the footwells and at the lower windscreen by the CABIN HT control mounted on the lower right instrument panel. In addition there are ducts leading to outlets at floor level at the front door posts, these outlets supply heated air to the rear cabin area. The cabin heat control is pulled out to select heat, and pushed in to turn the heat off. There is also a CABIN AIR control which opens a small door in the right forward fuselage side to provide fresh air through the same outlets. This air mixes with the heated air to provide a comfortable temperature.

The cabin heat system is very effective once the engine is warm, although its use is governed by a couple of safety factors.

The external scoop for the cabin air, opened by the cabin air control.

Firstly the heating system effectively opens a path through the firewall between the engine compartment and the cockpit. For this reason the cabin heat is selected OFF before engine start, or if fire is suspected in the engine compartment.

Secondly with a system of this type there is always a danger of Carbon Monoxide (CO) being introduced into the cabin. Carbon Monoxide is a gas produced as a by product of the combustion process. CO is colourless, odourless and tasteless, but its effects are potentially fatal. A generally accepted practice is to shut off the heating system if engine fumes (which may contain CO) are thought to be entering the cockpit. The danger arises if a crack or split is present in the exhaust system inside the heating shroud allowing carbon monoxide to enter the heating system.

The right side cockpit vent is fitted with an outside air temperature gauge.

The ventilation system consists of two cockpit vents, to the extreme right and left of the upper windscreen, which control fresh air from their respective external air intakes located in the inner wing leading edges. The cockpit vents are pulled out to allow fresh air to enter the cockpit, and can be rotated to direct the blast of air they provide. It is generally recommended that the vents be rotated to direct the air onto the inside of the windscreen, rather than directly into the face.

When the heating system is in use it is recommended that the fresh air vents be used to give a comfortable temperature mix. Doing so will help to combat the possible danger of carbon monoxide poisoning, and on a more mundane level will stop the cabin becoming 'stuffy' and possibly inducing drowsiness in the pilot.

Seats and Harnesses

The front seats may be adjustable four or six ways depending on the option fitted. For fore and aft positioning a bar located under the front edge of the seat cushion is raised, and the seat can be slid forward or back along the seat tracks until the desired position is reached. The handle is then released and the seat should be locked in position. Generally entry to and exit from the front seats is easiest with the seats in the rearmost position. Conversely to reach the rear seats the front seats are best in the fully forward position. The front seat backs may be adjusted for rake, and can be folded forward to allow easy access to the rear seats. Sixway adjustable seats have a crank at the outboard edge to adjust seat back rake, and a crank at the inboard edge to adjust seat height.

The rear seats may have one piece backs, with three possible positions, or two piece adjustable individually through almost infinite positions. Exact details and operation vary between different models, so it is best to familiarise oneself with the particular seat fitted.

The front seat design of the 172 has been subject to criticism regarding the security of the mechanism that locks the seat on the seat rail in the desired fore/aft position. The scenario is that when adjusted the seat fails to lock properly, undetected by the pilot. Then at some stage of flight (often just after take off) the seat runs rearward on the rails, taking the occupant with it. The possible consequences - especially if the pilot is flying solo, or if the controls are not released as the seat slides back - can be imagined. Prevention being the best cure, it is vital to positively ensure that the seat is locked in position, not only after adjustment but also as part of the pre-take off checks. The problem is usually well known to those with some experience on these types, but 30' high just after take off is not a good place to find out for the first time.

Harness design may vary between different aircraft and different options. The lap straps are all fixed to the frame via fittings on the floor, and are adjustable on the outboard strap. Shoulder straps for the front seats are usually stowed in a plastic channel above the cabin door, with an attachment point to the rear door post. The shoulder strap is fitted to the lap strap by snapping the link onto the lap strap stud. The shoulder strap is also adjustable once fixed to the lap strap. Use of the shoulder strap should be considered mandatory, as upper torso restraint has been shown to be a major factor in accident survivability. Final adjustment of the harness should be done when the seat is in the desired location.

Where a combined lap/shoulder strap with inertia reel is fitted care should be taken to ensure that the proper harness is being used for each seat as the harnesses cross from the attachment points in the centre cabin ceiling.

The baggage area behind the rear seats is accessible from the rear seats or from the external baggage door on the left side. Maximum baggage to be carried in this area is

120 lbs (54 Kg). The baggage area is sub-divided into two sections, one from behind the rear seats to the rear cabin bulkhead, and the other aft of the rear cabin bulkhead. A net and tie down straps and tie down rings are provided for securing baggage.

No more than 50 lbs (22 Kg) of baggage should be placed in the rear baggage compartment. All weight in either area

Detail of the front seat locking mechanism.

should be evenly distributed. Attention should be drawn to the weight and balance implications of weight in this area, it also must be remembered that for operations in the utility category the carriage of baggage is prohibited.

The rear baggage compartment, aft of the baggage door.

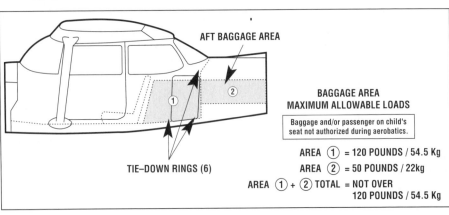

AFT BAGGAGE AREA

BAGGAGE AREA
MAXIMUM ALLOWABLE LOADS

Baggage and/or passenger on child's seat not authorized during aerobatics.

TIE–DOWN RINGS (6)

AREA ① = 120 POUNDS / 54.5 Kg
AREA ② = 50 POUNDS / 22kg
AREA ① + ② TOTAL = NOT OVER 120 POUNDS / 54.5 Kg

Doors And Windows

The 172 has a door each side of the cabin to allow for easy access. To close the door it is pulled shut, and to lock the door the the lever in the door armrest is moved forward to the horizontal position. To open the door the handle is pulled up and back to just past the vertical position, and the door will open. A door stop is fitted under each wing to stop the cabin doors from opening too far and damaging the hinges. The lockable baggage door in the rear left fuselage should be closed and locked during the pre-flight checks.

Although it is important for the doors to be properly latched for flight, the consequences of partial cabin door opening in flight are usually not serious. Where accidents do occur after a door opening in-flight, they are often caused by pilot distraction rather than as a direct

The baggage door.

result of the open door. If a door does open in flight it should be possible to close it by trimming the aircraft to approx 75 Knots, and slamming the door shut.

The cabin door, with the lever in the 'un-locked' position.

The cabin door lever down, to lock the door.

The window of the left hand door can be opened in flight (one of the factors that makes the 172 very popular for aerial photography). The small lever at the centre base of the window is moved clockwise a quarter turn to the vertical, and the window opens outward. In normal flight the airflow and slipstream should keep the window open, almost touching the lower surface of the wing. Sudden reductions in power should be avoided, as the window may close suddenly without warning. There will also be some temporary fluctuations in the readings of the pressure instruments as the window is opened. The aircraft can be flown with the window open at any speed up to VNE, however it is advisable to slow the aircraft below the normal cruise speed to reduce the wind noise and draught in the cabin.

Visibility through the windows can be degraded by oil smears, bugs and other matter accumulating on the windows. For window cleaning a soft cloth and warm, soapy water is recommended. The use of petrol, alcohol, thinners and window cleaner sprays is not recommended. On the subject of visibility it is common practice on the 172, as with other high wing aircraft, to lift a wing slightly before a turn in that direction - ie lift the left wing a couple of degrees to check for traffic before turning to the left.

The Cessna 172

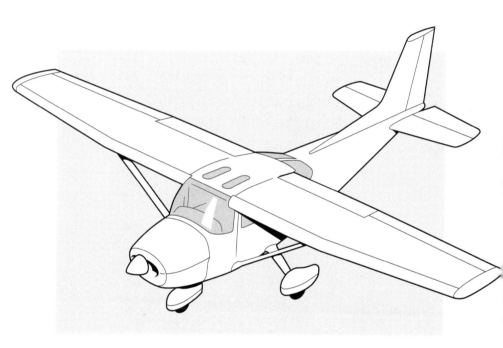

Limitations

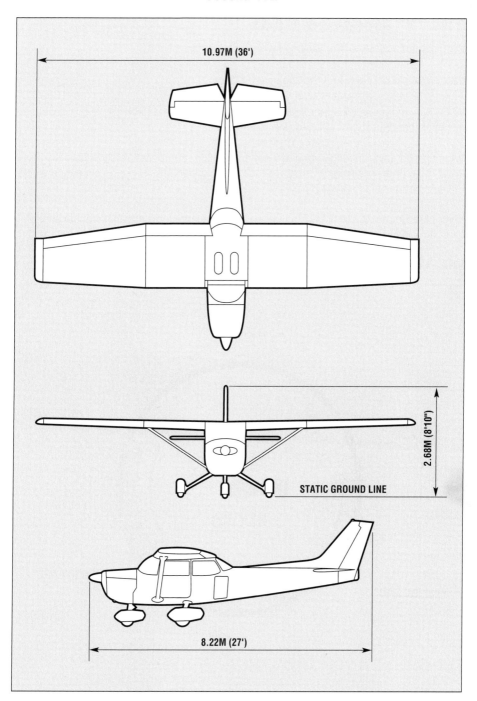

10.97M (36')

2.68M (8'10")

STATIC GROUND LINE

8.22M (27')

The 'V' Airspeed Code

VS0 - (Bottom of white arc) Stalling speed with full flap.

VS1 - (Bottom of green arc) Stalling speed 0 flap.

VFE - Maximum airspeed with flaps extended. Do not extend flaps above this speed, or fly faster than this speed with any flap extended.

VA - Design manoeuvring speed. Do not make full or abrupt control movements when flying faster than this speed. Design manoeuvring speed should not be exceeded when flying in turbulent conditions.

VNO - Maximum structural cruising speed. Do not exceed this speed except in smooth air conditions.

VNE - Never exceed speed. Do not exceed this airspeed under any circumstances

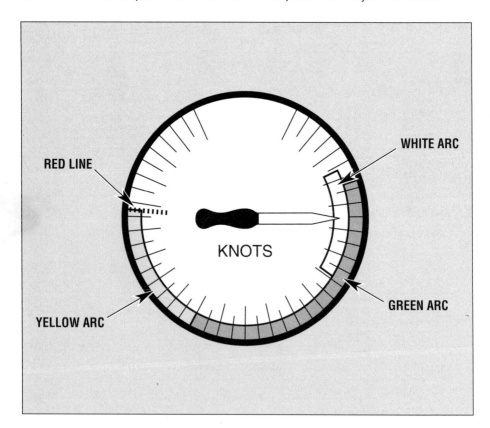

Cessna 172 Limitations

Airspeed Limitations - Cessna 172N 1976-78

(all quoted speeds are INDICATED airspeed-IAS)

	KNOTS	MPH	KPH
VNE	160	184	296
VNO	128	147	237
VA	97	112	180
VFE	85	98	158
Stalling Speed clean	47	54	87
Stalling Speed Full Flap	41	47	76

Airspeed Indicator Markings

RED LINE (Never Exceed)	160	184	296
YELLOW ARC (Caution range)	128 - 160	147 - 184	237 - 296
GREEN ARC (Normal operating range)	47 - 128	54 - 147	87 - 237
WHITE ARC (Flap extended range)	41 - 85	47 - 98	76 - 158

Maximum Demonstrated Crosswind Component

15 Knots

Airspeed Limitations - Cessna 172N 1979-81

(quoted speeds are INDICATED airspeed-IAS)

	KNOTS	MPH	KPH
VNE	158	182	293
VNO	127	146	235
VA	97	112	180
VFE (10°)	110	127	204
VFE (10° - 40°)	85	98	158
Stalling Speed clean	44	50	82
Stalling Speed Full Flap	33	38	61

Airspeed Indicator Markings

RED LINE (Never Exceed)	158	182	293
YELLOW ARC (Caution range)	127 - 158	146 - 182	235 - 293
GREEN ARC (Normal operating range)	44 - 127	50 - 146	82 - 235
WHITE ARC (Flap extended range)	33 - 85	38 - 98	61 - 158

Maximum Demonstrated Crosswind Component   15 Knots

Airspeed Limitations Cessna 172P 1981-1985

(all quoted speeds are INDICATED airspeed-IAS)

	KNOTS	MPH	KPH
VNE	158	182	293
VNO	127	146	235
VA (in utility category)	102 @ 2100lbs		
VA (at 2400 lb)	99	144	183
VA (at 2000 lb)	92	106	170
VA (at 1600 lb)	82	94	152
VFE (10°)	110	127	204
VFE (10°-30°)	85	98	158
Stalling Speed clean	44	50	82
Stalling Speed Full Flap	33	38	61

Airspeed Indicator Markings

RED LINE (Never Exceed)	158	182	293
YELLOW ARC (Caution range)	127 - 158	146 - 182	235 - 293
GREEN ARC (Normal operating range)	44 - 127	50 - 146	82 - 235
WHITE ARC (Flap extended range)	33 - 85	38 - 98	61 - 158

Maximum Demonstrated Crosswind Component   15 Knots

Airframe Limitations C172N

WEIGHTS	NORMAL		UTILITY	
	lbs	Kg	lbs	Kg
Maximum Take Off Weight	2300	1043	2000	907
Maximum Landing Weight	2300	1043	2000	907
Maximum Baggage Weight	120	54	0	0

Flight Load Factors

	Normal	Utility
Max Positive load factor:		
FLAPS UP	3.8G	4.4G
FLAPS DOWN	3.0G	3.0G
Max Negative load factor:		
FLAPS UP	-1.52	-1.76

Performance Limitations

Service Ceiling - 14200 ft

Airframe Limitations C172P

WEIGHTS	NORMAL		UTILITY	
	lbs	Kg	lbs	Kg
Maximum Ramp Weight	2407	1092	2107	956
Maximum Take Off Weight	2400	1088	2100	952
Maximum Landing Weight	2400	1088	2100	952
Maximum Baggage Weight	120	54	0	0

Flight Load Factors

	Normal	Utility
Max Positive load factor:		
FLAPS UP	3.8G	4.4G
FLAPS DOWN	3.0G	3.0G
Max Negative load factor:		
FLAPS UP	-1.52	-1.76

Performance Limitations

Service Ceiling - 13000 ft

Engine Limitations C172N

	Tachometer	Instrument Marking
Maximum RPM	2700	Red Line
Normal Operating Range	2200 - 2700	Green Arc

	Oil Temperature	Instrument Marking
Normal operating range	up to 245°F	Green Arc
Maximum	245°F / 118°C	Red Line

	Oil Pressure	Instrument Marking
Normal operating range	60 - 90 psi	Green Arc
Minimum	25 psi	Red Line
Maximum	100 psi	Red Line

Oil Quantity

	US quart	Litre
Note: dipstick is marked in US quarts		
Capacity	6	5.7
Minimum safe quantity	4	3.8

Fuel System

Fuel Quantity - Standard Tanks	US Gal	Imp Gal	Litre
Note: cockpit fuel gauges are marked in US gallons			
Total Capacity	43	36	163
Unusable Fuel	3	2.5	11
Usable Fuel (all flight conditions)	40	33	152

Miscellaneous Limitations C172N

Nose Wheel Tyre Pressure	31 psi	2.14 bar (5.00 X 5)
Main Wheel Tyre Pressure	29 psi	2.00 bar (6.00 X 6)

Engine Limitations C172P

	Tachometer	Instrument Marking
Maximum RPM	2700	Red Line
Normal Operating Range	2100 - 2700	Green Arc

	Oil Temperature	Instrument Marking
Normal operating range	100 - 245°F	Green Arc
Maximum	245°F / 118°C	Red Line

	Oil Pressure	Instrument Marking
Normal operating range	60 - 90 psi	Green Arc
Minimum	25 psi	Red Line
Maximum	115 psi	Red Line

Oil Quantity

	US quart	Litre
Note: dipstick is marked in US quarts		
Sump Capacity	7	6.6
Minimum safe quantity	5	4.7

Fuel System

Fuel Quantity - Standard Tanks	US Gal	Imp Gal	Litre
Note: cockpit fuel gauges are marked in US gallons			
Total Capacity	43	36	163
Unusable Fuel	3	2.5	11
Usable Fuel (all flight conditions)	40	33	152

Miscellaneous Limitations C172P

Nose Wheel Tyre Pressure	34 psi	2.35 bar (5.00 X 5)
Main Wheel Tyre Pressure	28 psi	1.95 bar (6.00 X 6)

Oil Grades

Lycoming approve lubricating oil for the engine that conforms to specification MIL-L-6082 (straight mineral type) and specification MIL-L-22851 (ashless dispersant type).

Straight mineral type - known mostly as straight oil - is usually only used when the engine is new, or after maintenance work on the engine. Straight oil grades are known by their number - ie 80, 100.

Ashless dispersant oils are more commonly used in service. These oil grades carry the prefix 'W', ie W80, W100. Ashless dispersant type - 'W' oil - must not be used where the engine is operating on straight oil, nor can 'W' oil be added to straight mineral oil. It is therefore very important to check which type of oil is currently being used in the engine, and be sure only to add the same type.

Both types of oil are available in different grades, used according to the average ground air temperature. The recommended grades are set out as SAE numbers, but available in commercial grade numbers - which are different! Thankfully the situation is more simple than it appears, to get the approximate commercial grade, double the SAE number, ie SAE 50 = commercial grade 100 (or W100). The table below shows the recommended grades for various surface temperature bands.

AVERAGE SURFACE AIR TEMPERATURE	MIL-L-6082 Straight mineral	COMMERCIAL GRADE
Above 60°F / 16°C	SAE 50	100
30°F / -1°C - 90°F / 32°C	SAE 40	80
0°F / -18°C - 70°F / 21°C	SAE 30	65
Below 10°F / -12°C	SAE 20	55
AVERAGE SURFACE AIR TEMPERATURE	**MIL-L-22851 Ashless Dispersant**	**COMMERCIAL GRADE**
Above 60°F / 16°C	SAE 50 or SAE 40	W100 or W80
30°F / -1°C - 90°F / 32°C	SAE 40	W80
0°F / -18°C - 70°F / 21°C	SAE 30 or SAE 40	W65 or W80
Below 10°F / -12°C	SAE 30	W65
* also SAE 20W-50 approved for all temperatures		

Fuel Grades

The Cessna 172 is certified for use with 100LL fuels.

The table below shows the recommended fuel grades. It is wise to pay attention when your aircraft is being refuelled, especially if at an airfield new to you. More than one pilot has found out to their cost that piston engines designed for AVGAS do not run very well on AVTUR (Jet A-1). To help guard against this eventuality AVGAS fuelling points carry a RED sticker, and AVTUR fuelling points a BLACK sticker. The C-172P may also use Mogas (motor gasoline) ie. 4 Star petrol – in accordance with detailed limitations and restrictions set out by the CAA in an Airworthiness Notice.

APPROVED FUEL GRADES

100LL

100L

100 (formerly 100/130)

The Cessna 172

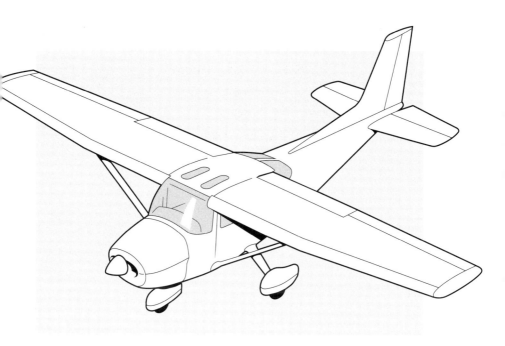

Handling The Cessna 172

Note: *The information in this section is no substitute for flying instruction under the guidance of a flying instructor familiar with the aircraft and its characteristics.*

Ground Handling

Whenever possible a towbar should be used for manually manoeuvring the aircraft. The towbar attaches to the nosewheel assembly, and provides a point to push or pull as well as allowing accurate steering. When using a towbar take care not to exceed the nosewheel turning angle limit of 30°

Unfortunately a towbar is not always available when you need it. In this case the push/pulling points are the wing strut ends and undercarriage legs. Using the propeller to pull or push is very much a matter of personal choice - bearing in mind that it is virtually impossible to be sure that the propellor is not 'LIVE' - even with the keys out of the magneto switch. The leading edge of the tailplane MUST NOT be used as a pushing point - there are recorded cases of structural damage to the tailplane caused by incorrect ground handling. To steer the aircraft without a towbar, the tail must be lowered to raise the nosewheel clear of the ground, the aircraft can then be pivoted about the main wheels. The tail can be lowered by pushing down over the

tailplane front spar adjacent to the fuselage, or over a rear fuselage bulkhead. DO NOT push down on the outer tailplane or on the control surfaces. The aircraft flying instructor or operator should be able to point out the correct push down points.

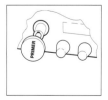

Engine Starting

Starting of the 172 is straightforward, the ambient conditions and engine temperature being the principal factors to be considered. Somewhere between 2 and 6 primes are required for starting, generally the colder the ambient temperature and engine temperature, the more priming will be required. The throttle is set to 1/4" open (that is 1/4 in), 'pumping' of the throttle, especially during starting, should be avoided.

Cranking of the starter should be limited to 30 seconds at a time due to the danger of the starter motor overheating. That said, 30 seconds is a bit extreme, and if the engine does not fire within 10-15 seconds you can reasonably suppose that something is amiss (usually the engine is over or under primed). After a prolonged period of engine cranking without a successful start the starter should be allowed a few minutes to cool before a further starting attempt is made. The starter should not be operated after engine start as damage to the starter may result. The starter warning light should go out after engine start, if it remains lit the engine should be shut down without delay.

After start the oil pressure should register within 30 seconds (or slightly longer in very cold conditions), should the oil pressure not register the engine should be shut down without delay. Readings on the suction gauge and ammeter are also checked after engine start.

To check proper operation of the fuel system the engine should be started on one tank (Left or Right), and then set to the opposite tank for taxying. The power checks and take-off must be made with fuel selector set to Both.

Starting With a Suspected Flooded Engine

An overprimed (flooded) engine will be indicated by weak intermittent firing, and puffs of black smoke from the exhaust during the attempted start. If it is suspected that the engine is flooded (over primed) the throttle should be opened fully and the mixture moved to idle cut off. If the engine starts the throttle should be retarded to the normal position and the mixture moved to fully rich.

Starting In Cold Ambient Conditions (below 0°c)

Failure to start due to an underprimed engine is more likely to occur in cold conditions with a cold engine. An underprimed engine will not fire at all, and additional priming is necessary. Starting in cold temperatures will be more difficult due to several factors. The oil will be more viscous, the battery may lose up to half of its capacity and the fuel will not vaporise readily. A greater number of primes will be required as discussed above, external power may be needed to supplement the aircraft battery, and pre-heat may be necessary in very low temperatures.

Taxying

In the first few feet of taxying a brake check is normally carried out, followed by steering and differential brake checks in due course. To anyone used to aircraft with 'direct' steering rods from the rudder pedals to the nose wheel the spring link system of the 172 may at first seem a little 'loose' and inexact. It should be remembered that the rudder pedals only steer the nosewheel through 10° either side of neutral, and differential braking is required to castor the nose wheel to its limit of 30°.

However the 172 is easy to taxy, although practice may be needed in the increased use of the rudder pedals and differential braking when taxying in crosswind conditions.

When taxying with a crosswind 'opposite rudder' will be required, up to full deflection i.e. with a crosswind from the left, up to full right rudder may be required as the aircraft tries to 'weathercock' into wind.

The chart below shows recommended control wheel positions when taxying with the prevailing wind from the directions shown.

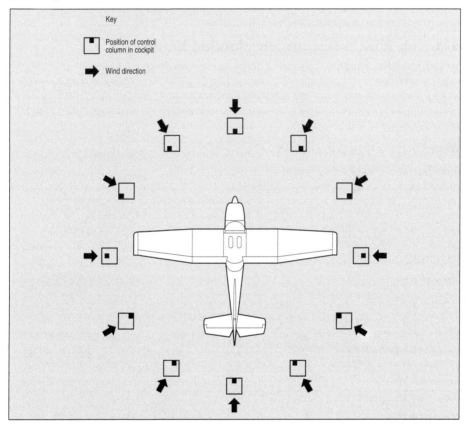

Speed control is important, especially when taxying over rough surfaces or in strong wind conditions. When slowing the aircraft the throttle should always be closed first, and then the brakes evenly applied to slow the aircraft. When taxying over loose stones or gravel the RPM should be kept to an absolute minimum to avoid propeller damage.

Prolonged idling (below about 800 rpm) should be avoided during ground operations as it can lead to plug fouling

Power and Pre-Take-off Checks

The aircraft is usually positioned into wind to aid engine cooling, and before the power check starts the oil temperature should be in the green arc, and the fuel selector should be set to Both.

The engine is generally run up to 1700 RPM, and the carburettor heat is checked, a small drop in rpm should result. The subject of carb. icing is covered more fully later, however an important point to note is that the inlet for the 'hot' air is unfiltered, and so dust, grass etc. may well enter the engine when 'hot' air is selected, leading to increased engine wear. For this reason the use of carb. heat should be kept to the minimum necessary whilst on the ground.

The magnetos are checked individually, a small drop in RPM (no more than 125 RPM) is the norm and shows that the ignition system is functioning properly. No drop at all in RPM when operating on one magneto may well indicate a malfunction in the ignition system, and the possibility that one or both magnetos is staying 'live'. RPM should not vary between each single magneto by more than 50 RPM. An excessive drop in RPM when operating on one magneto, especially when accompanied by rough running, may indicate fouled spark plugs or a faulty magneto. If fouled plugs are suspected it may be possible to clear the problem. The engine is advanced to about 2000 RPM with magnetos on 'BOTH', and the mixture leaned to give the 'peak' RPM. This should be held for about 10 seconds, then the mixture is returned to fully rich, power is brought back to 1700 RPM and the magnetos can be rechecked.

> **WARNING:** Excessive power setting and over lean mixture settings should be avoided during this procedure. If the problem does not clear the aircraft should be considered unserviceable.

The engine gauges are checked at 1700 RPM for normal indications, together with the suction gauge and ammeter.

Engine idling is also checked, with the throttle closed the engine should run smoothly at about 500 - 750 rpm.

During the pre-takeoff checks particular attention should be paid to the security of the front seats on their tracks. The problem of front seat security has already been covered at length and before take-off is the time to check your seat, it may be too late once you are airborne.

Take-off

Normally take-off is made with the mixture in the fully RICH position. At high elevation airfields (above say 3000' AMSL) it may be necessary to lean the mixture before take-off to give full power. The fuel selector should be in the 'Both' position for take-off (as for the power and pre-take-off checks).

For all take-offs care must be taken to ensure that the feet remain clear of the toe brakes, this is best done by keeping the heels on the floor. Inadvertent pressure on the toe brakes can significantly slow the aircraft during the take-off run, and lead to directional control difficulties.

At the start of the take-off run (as at all other times), the throttle should be opened smoothly and progressively. Rapid opening of the throttle should specifically be avoided at all times. The normal rotate speed is around 55 knots, with a climb speed of around 75 knots dependent on conditions and operator procedures. For 'short field' take-offs the use of 10° of flap is common practice. Flap settings beyond 10° must not be used for take-off as the increased lift is matched by a larger increase in drag and so is counterproductive. It should be appreciated that the use of 10° of flap may degrade the climb performance in high density altitude conditions at high gross weights.

On rough surfaces particularly it is important to protect the nose wheel by keeping weight off it during the take-off run, through use of the elevator. Care should be taken to avoid 'over-rotating' during the take-off run as this will lengthen the take-off run (and ruin the view ahead!).

Climbing

An airspeed in the region of 75 knots will give the best rate of climb after takeoff, the exact figure varies between models - check the aircraft flight manual. The best angle of climb (the best increase in height for the shortest distance travelled over the ground) is obtained at about 60 knots. With 10° of flaps set Cessna recommend an obstacle clearance speed of 56 knots. During climbing it is important to monitor the engine gauges, as the engine is operating at a high power setting but with a reduced cooling airflow compared to cruising flight. Lookout ahead is impaired by the high nose attitude, and it is common practice to 'weave' the nose periodically during the climb to visually check the area ahead. Both the best rate of climb and best angle of climb airspeeds reduce as altitude increases - details will be found in the flight manuals of later model aircraft.

Cruising Flight

Cruising is normally done with a power setting of 55-75%. Typically a setting of about 2200 RPM will give an indicated airspeed of around 105 knots.

If turbulent conditions are encountered in flight, particular care must be taken not to exceed the Va (Design Manoeuvring Speed). The Va speed differs between the 172N and 172P. For the 172N a Va of 97 knots IAS is quoted. For the 172P Va is quoted for various gross weights:

172P

2400 lbs 99 Knots IAS

2000 lbs 92 Knots IAS

1600 lbs 82 Knots IAS

Engine Handling

Engine rough running can be caused by a number of factors, it should be remembered that the majority of engine failures in light aircraft are caused by pilot error. After carburettor icing, fuel exhaustion (running out of fuel) and fuel starvation (ie running one tank dry) feature as causes of engine failures on 172s.

Having sufficient fuel on board to complete the flight is a point of basic airmanship, and mostly accomplished through proper flight planning and thorough pre-flight checks - especially a VISUAL check of fuel tank contents. Proper in-flight checks should ensure adequate monitoring of the fuel system. For cruising the fuel selector can be in the 'Left', 'Both', or 'Right' position. With the fuel selector in the 'Left' or 'Right' position care should be taken to keep the fuel tank levels approximately even and not to run one tank completely dry.

Regular monitoring of the engine instruments may forewarn of an impending problem. HIGH OIL TEMPERATURE, if not accompanied by a corresponding drop in oil pressure, may indicate a faulty gauge. As with most instances the action to be taken will depend on the pilot's judgement of the situation at the time. As general guidance a diversion to a suitable airfield, whilst remaining alert to the possibility of a sudden engine failure, would make a reasonable course of action. ***Where high oil temperature is accompanied by a low oil pressure, engine failure may very well be imminent, and the pilot should act accordingly.*** Such a situation might occur during a prolonged slow climb in hot conditions, in this instance increasing the airspeed to provide more cooling, and reducing power if possible may restore oil temperature to normal. In the event of a LOW OIL PRESSURE reading, accompanied by a normal oil temperature reading, again gauge failure may be the culprit, and the pilot can consider actions similar to those for an oil temperature gauge failure. Where the low oil pressure is accompanied by a high oil temperature, engine failure could well be imminent and the pilot will want to act accordingly.

Stalling

Note: *The information in this section is no substitute for flying instruction under the guidance of a flying instructor familiar with the aircraft and its characteristics.*

The 172 is conventional in its stalling behaviour, indeed at light weights and forward c.g. positions (as with the utility category) it can be quite difficult to achieve a full stall .The horn stall warning activates 5 to 10 knots above the stall airspeed, the airspeed indicator is unreliable near to stall airspeeds and tends to under read considerably. The use of power will lower the stalling speed, whilst turning flight raises the stall speed. With the flaps down some elevator buffeting occurs prior to the stall, the use of flaps, power or turning flight considerably increases the chances of a wing drop at the stall. When practising stalls the possibility of a wing drop can be reduced by keeping the aircraft in balance during the approach to the stall. Typical height loss for a full stall with a conventional recovery (using power) is about 200'.

Spins

Note: *The information in this section is no substitute for flying instruction under the guidance of a flying instructor familiar with the aircraft and its characteristics.*

Cessna produce a supplement detailing the spinning characteristics and recovery procedures for the single engine Cessna aircraft. It is highly recommended that you study this supplement before any intentional spinning.

The Cessna 172 is approved for intentional spinning ONLY when operating in the utility category, however

INTENTIONAL SPINS WITH FLAPS EXTENDED ARE PROHIBITED

In addition no baggage is to be carried and the rear seats are not to be occupied.

As with stalling several factors can affect the behaviour of the aircraft in the spin. It is quite possible to devote a whole book just to this subject, and it is not the intention here to write a text book on spinning, however some points are worthy of mention. The weight of the aircraft (and particularly the c.g. position) has a noticeable effect on the spin, a forward c.g. position makes a pure spin more difficult to obtain, a spiral with increasing airspeed and 'G' loads is more likely. With aft c.g. positions the spin is easier to achieve, and recoveries may take longer. High weights tend to extend the spin recovery due to the increase in inertia. The use of power in the spin tends to lead to a 'flatter' spin attitude, and recoveries may be lengthened. Finally the position of the ailerons is important in spinning. The ailerons should be held NEUTRAL through out the spin and recovery.

Cessna realise the difficulty of entering a spin with the 172 operating in the utility category, unless a little power is used in the spin entry. Even when this technique is used the 172 exhibits spiral tendencies, and will usually spiral out of a spin within 2-3 turns, without establishing in a steady spin. Recovery is just about instantaneous once the recovery actions are taken. The reluctance of the 172 to spin is a very positive point in favour of an aeroplane that is, after all, designed as a touring aircraft rather than a trainer.

The Cessna recommended spin recovery action can be summarised as:
- Check ailerons neutral and throttle closed
- Apply and maintain full opposite rudder (opposite to the direction of spin)
- Just after the rudder reaches the stop move the control wheel briskly forward until the stall is broken and the spin stops.
- When rotation stops centralise the rudder, and recover from the ensuing dive.

Cessna make the point that in the event of an inadvertent spin (ie probably outside of the utility category limitations), an aft c.g. loading may mean that the control wheel has to be held fully forward - ie fully down elevator - to assure spin recovery.

Descent

The descent may be powered or glide, for the glide a speed of 65 knots is recommended. Where flaps are used the rate of descent increases markedly. The initial lowering of flap leads to a distinct nose up pitching and reduced airspeed. Especially at airspeeds close to VFE the trim change can be quite marked and the aircraft may 'balloon' whilst the attitude is changed and the aircraft re-trimmed. Cessna do not recommend side slipping with flaps extended beyond 20° due to aerodynamic buffeting of the tail surfaces. Most operators discourage sideslipping with any flap extended, apart from other considerations the 172 can take on a very high rate of descent in a glide with flaps extended, the additional descent rate caused by sideslipping can prove excessive when close to the ground.

The low power settings usually used during the descent, and a possible prolonged descent into warmer air, provide ideal conditions for carburettor icing. Full carburettor heat should be used where necessary, and in a glide descent power should be added for short periods throughout the descent to help prevent plug fouling, rapid cylinder cooling and of course carb. icing.

Landing

The Cessna 172 is almost universally regarded as being an easy aircraft to land. However in common with most light aircraft the 172 has an Achilles Heel in the form of the relative weakness of the nose gear. As the 172 is not as commonly used for basic training the incidence of landing accidents is lower than for the 150 and 152s. However accidents do occur and the accident reports tend to read much the same:

"Cessna F172 ——-. (Distraction).. caused the pilot to make a heavy landing during which the nose gear collapsed."

"Cessna F172M ——-. Nose gear collapsed following a pilot-induced oscillation on landing...."

"Reims Cessna F172N ——-. Nose landing gear and firewall bulkhead damaged by three bounces on landing ....."

As already covered the nosewheel is nowhere near as strong as the main undercarriage, but there is no need for its strength to be tested if a proper approach and landing technique is used. Approach speed for a normal approach with flap is about 70 knots, usually a little higher for a flapless approach, dependent on conditions and operator procedures. A short field approach is made at 60 knots (172N) / 61 knots (172P) with full flap. Incorrect approach speed is a primary cause of 'ballooning', which often leads to bouncing. Bouncing also arises where the aircraft is allowed to touch down at too high a speed, usually in a level attitude rather than a nose up attitude. The correct action in either a 'balloon' or a bounce is to GO AROUND without delay.

The correct landing technique is to approach at the proper speed, 'flare' or 'hold off', close the throttle and gradually raise the nose to ensure a low touch down speed on the MAINWHEELS FIRST, with the nose wheel still off the ground. As the aircraft slows down correct use of the elevators means the nose wheel is allowed to gently contact the surface some time after the initial mainwheel contact. Again there is no substitute for flying instruction in the proper technique with a flying instructor.

The correct landing attitude may be more difficult to achieve when full flap is extended (particularly when full flap is 40° as on the 172N), the aircraft will tend to land 'flat'. In a glide approach with full flap the high rate of descent and large change in attitude required to flare takes some getting used to.

One of the significant airframe modifications between the 172N and 172P was the reduction in maximum flap setting from 40° to 30°. This act was not universally welcomed, as in the right hands 40° of flap on the 172N could prove very useful at times. However limiting the flap to 30° does simplify the full flap go-around procedure.

The go around with full flap in the 172 is characterised by a considerable trim change when full power is applied, and some pilots may have difficulty in holding the attitude required until able to use the elevator trimmer to reduce the control force. One of the immediate actions in the go-around is to raise the flaps to 20° to improve climb performance. With 40° flap extended on the 172N the climb performance near to max. gross weight leaves a lot to be desired, and the use of 40° flap should be reserved for occasions when it is really required.

Parking and Tie Down

The aircraft is generally parked into wind, it is good practice to stop with the nosewheel straight so that the rudder is not deflected. All switches should be off, the doors closed and the control lock fitted. In extremely cold weather it may advisable NOT to set the parking brake as moisture may freeze the brakes, also the parking brake should not be set if there is reason to believe that the brakes are overheated. If for any reason the parking brake is not set the wheels should be 'chocked'.

When strong winds are forecast, all possible precautions should be taken.

When tying down the aircraft the following technique is recommended:

● Park aircraft into wind with the control wheel lock in.

● Ropes, cables or chains are attached to the wing tie down points and secured to ground anchor points.

● If desired a rope (not cable or chain) can be secured to the exposed portion of the engine mount and secured to a ground anchor point.

● A rope can be passed through the tail tie down point and each end secured at 45° angle to the ground each side of the tail.

● Fitting of external control locks (particularly to the rudder) may be advisable in strong or gusty wind conditions.

It is also prudent to use a pitot cover, particularly if the aircraft will be left unattended for some time.

The Cessna 172

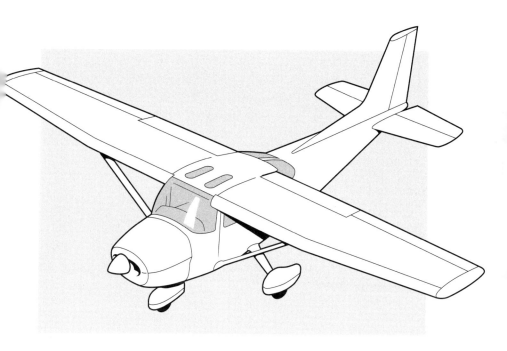

Mixture And Carb Icing Supplement

MIXTURE AND CARB. ICING SUPPLEMENT.

Carburettor Icing

Almost certainly the most common cause of engine rough running, and complete engine failures, is carburettor icing. Despite this carburettor icing remains a widely misunderstood subject, with many pilots' knowledge of the subject being limited to a feeling that the carb heat should be used regularly in flight, without really knowing the symptoms of carb. icing or the conditions most likely to cause its formation.

How Carburettor Icing Forms

IMPACT ICING occurs when ice forms over the external air inlet (air filter) and inside the induction system leading to the carburettor. This type of icing occurs with the temperature below 0°C whilst flying in cloud, or in precipitation (ie rain, sleet or snow). These conditions are also conducive to airframe icing, and this aircraft is NOT CLEARED FOR FLIGHT INTO KNOWN ICING CONDITIONS, which clearly these are. So, assuming the aircraft is operated legally within its limitations, this form of icing should not occur, and is not considered further.

CARBURETTOR ICING is caused by a temperature drop inside the carburettor, which can happen even in conditions where other forms of icing will not occur. The causes of this temperature drop are twofold:

1. Fuel Icing - the evaporation of fuel inside the carburettor. Liquid fuel changes to fuel vapour and mixes with the induction air causing a large temperature drop. If the temperature inside the carburettor falls below 0°C, water vapour in the atmosphere condenses into ice, usually on the walls of the carburettor passage adjacent to the fuel jet, and on the throttle valve. Generally fuel icing is responsible for around 70% of the temperature drop in the carburettor.

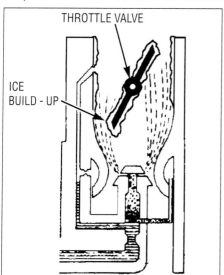

THROTTLE VALVE

ICE BUILD - UP

2. Throttle icing - the temperature loss caused by the acceleration of air and consequent pressure drop around the throttle valve. This effect may again take the temperature below 0°C, and water vapour in the inlet air will condense into ice on the throttle valve. This practical effect is a demonstration of Bernoulli's Principle.

As fuel and throttle icing generally occur together, they are considered just as carburettor icing.

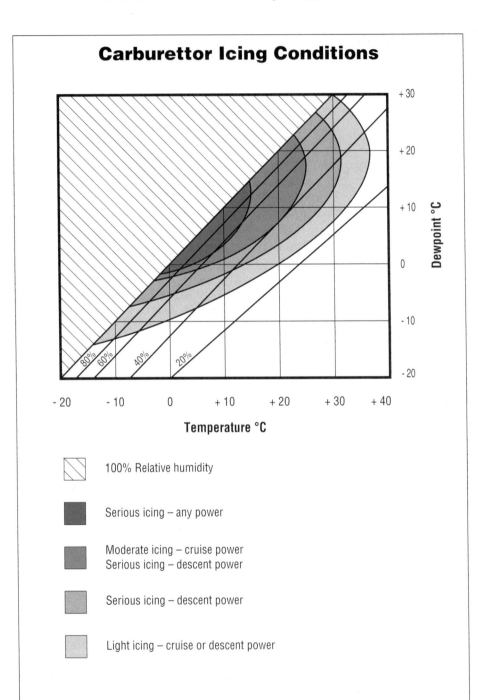

Carburettor Icing Conditions

100% Relative humidity

Serious icing – any power

Moderate icing – cruise power
Serious icing – descent power

Serious icing – descent power

Light icing – cruise or descent power

Conditions Likely To Lead To Carburettor Icing

Two criteria govern the likelihood of carburettor icing conditions, the AIR TEMPERATURE and the RELATIVE HUMIDITY.

The ambient air temperature is important, BUT NOT BECAUSE THE TEMPERATURE NEEDS TO BE BELOW 0°C, OR EVEN CLOSE TO FREEZING. The temperature drop in the carburettor can be up to 30°C, so carburettor icing can (and does) occur in hot ambient conditions. No wonder carburettor icing is sometimes referred to as refrigeration icing. Carburettor icing is considered a possibility within the temperature range of -10°C to +30°C.

The relative humidity (a measure of the water content of the atmosphere) is the major factor. The greater the water content in the atmosphere (the higher the relative humidity), the greater the risk of carburettor icing. That said the relative humidity (RH) does not to have to be 100% (ie visible water droplets - cloud, rain), for carburettor icing to occur. Carburettor icing is considered a possibility at relative humidity values as low as 30%, but it is rare that the RH gets this low in Europe. Herein lies the real danger of carburettor icing, that it can occur in such a wide range of conditions. Obviously the pilot must be alert to the possibility of carburettor icing at just about all times. Flight in or near cloud, or in other visible moisture (ie rain) might be an obvious cause of carburettor icing, but - VISIBLE MOISTURE DOES NOT NEED TO BE PRESENT FOR CARBURETTOR ICING TO OCCUR.

Symptoms Of Carburettor Icing

In this aircraft, fitted with a fixed pitch propeller, the symptoms of carburettor icing are straightforward. A loss of RPM will be the first symptom, although this is often first noticed as a loss of altitude. As the icing becomes more serious, engine rough running may occur.

Carburettor icing is often detected during the use of the carburettor heat. Normally when the carburettor heat is used, a small drop in rpm occurs, when the control is returned to cold (off) the rpm restores to the same as before the use of carburettor heat. If the rpm restores to a higher figure than before the carburettor heat was used, it can be reasonably supposed that some form of carburettor icing was present.

Use Of Carburettor Heat

Apart from the normal check of carburettor heat during the power checks, it may be necessary to use the carburettor heat on the ground if carburettor icing is suspected. Safety considerations apart, the use of carburettor heat on the ground should be kept to a minimum, as the hot air inlet is unfiltered, and so sand or dust can enter the engine, increasing engine wear.

Carburettor icing is generally considered to be very unlikely with the engine operating at above 75% power, ie during the take-off and climb. Carburettor heat should not be used with the engine operating at above 75% power (ie full throttle) as detonation may occur. Detonation is the uncontrolled burning of fuel in the cylinders, literally an explosion, and will cause serious damage to the engine very quickly. Apart from the danger of detonation, the use of carburettor heat reduces the power the engine produces. In any situation where full power is required (ie take-off, climb, go-around) the carburettor heat must be off (cold).

Very few operators recommend the use of anything other than FULL carburettor heat. A normal carburettor icing check will involve leaving the carburettor heat on (hot) for 5-10 seconds, although the pilot may wish to vary this dependent on the conditions. The use of carburettor heat does increase the fuel consumption, and this may be a factor to consider if the aircraft is being flown towards the limit of its range/endurance in possible carburettor icing conditions.

With carburettor icing present, the use of carburettor heat may lead to a large drop in rpm, with rough running. The instinctive reaction is to put the carburettor heat back to cold (off), and quickly. This is, however, the wrong action. Chances are this rough running is a good thing, and the carburettor heat should be left on (hot) until the rough running clears and the rpm rises. In this instance the use of carburettor heat has melted a large amount of accumulated icing and the melted ice is passing through the engine, causing temporary rough running.

Care should be taken when flying in very cold ambient conditions (below -10°C). In these conditions the use of carburettor heat may actually raise the temperature in the carburettor to that most conducive to carburettor icing. Generally when the temperature

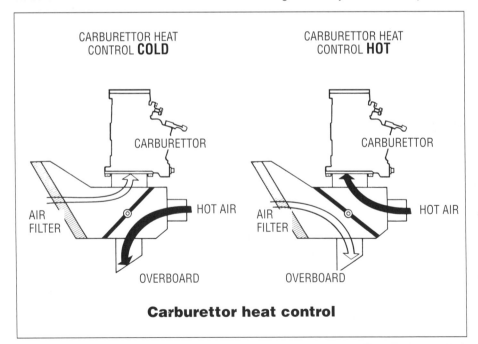

Carburettor heat control

© Airplan Flight Equipment 1993

in the carburettor is below -8°C moisture forms directly into ice crystals which pass through the engine.

The rpm loss normally associated with the use of carburettor heat is caused by the reduced density of the hot air entering the carburettor, leading to an over rich mixture entering the engine. If the carburettor heat has to be left constantly on (hot) - ie flight in heavy rain and cloud - it may be advisable to lean the mixture in order to maintain rpm and smooth engine running.

It is during the descent (and particularly the glide descent) that carburettor icing is most likely to occur. The position of the throttle valve (ie almost closed) is a contributory factor, and even though the carburettor heat is normally applied throughout a glide descent, the low engine power will reduce the temperature of the hot air selected with the carburettor heat control. In addition a loss of power may not be readily noticed. The propeller is likely to windmill even after a complete loss of power and so a full loss of power may only be apparent when the throttle is opened at the bottom of the descent. This is one good reason for opening the throttle to 'warm the engine' at intervals during a glide descent.

The Mixture Control

The aircraft is provided with a mixture control so that the pilot can adjust the fuel/air mixture entering the engine. The cockpit mixture control operates a needle valve between the float bowl and the main metering jet. This valve controls the fuel flow to the main metering jet to adjust the mixture, with the mixture control in the ICO position (fully lean) the valve is fully closed.

Reasons For Adjusting The Mixture

Correct leaning of the engine mixture will enable the engine to be operated at its most efficient in terms of fuel consumption. With the increased use of 100LL fuel, leaning is also important to reduce spark plug fouling.

The most efficient engine operation is obtained with a fuel/air ratio of about 1:15, that is 1 part fuel to 15 parts air. In fact with the mixture set to fully rich, the system is designed to give a slightly richer mixture than ideal, typically about 1:12. This slightly over rich mixture reduces the possibility of pre-ignition or detonation, and aids cylinder cooling.

As altitude increases the air density decreases. Above about 3000' the reduced air density can lead to an over rich mixture. If the mixture becomes excessively rich, power will be lost, rough running may be evident and ultimately engine failure will occur due to a 'rich cut'. It is for this reason that the mixture control is provided to ensure the correct fuel/air ratio, typically it is used when cruising above 3000'.

The flight manuals for some older aircraft recommend leaning only above 5000'. However with the increasing use of AVGAS 100LL, and the plug fouling problems sometimes associated with 100LL, most operators recommend leaning once above 3000'.

Effect of Mixture Adjustment

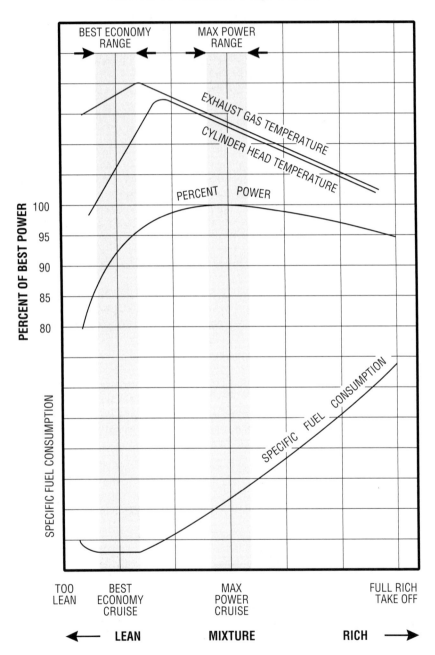

© Airplan Flight Equipment 1993

Use Of The Mixture Control

For take-off and climb the mixture should be fully rich, the only exception being operation from a high density altitude airport when leaning may be necessary to ensure the availability of max. power. On reaching a cruising altitude above about 3000' the cruise power should be set, and then leaning can be carried out (note: generally leaning with over 75% power set is not recommended). If climbing above about 5000', full throttle will be less than 75% power on a normally aspirated engine and so leaning may be permissible to maintain smooth running.

Assuming that there is no Exhaust Gas Temperature (EGT) gauge and no cylinder head temperature gauge, the primary instrument to watch when leaning is the RPM gauge (tachometer).

To lean the engine, the recommended power setting (RPM) is set with the throttle. Next, with a constant throttle setting, the mixture control is slowly moved back (leaned). If leaning is required the RPM will increase slowly, peak, and then decrease as the mixture is leaned, if leaning is continued the engine will ultimately run rough and lose power.

If the mixture is set to achieve peak RPM, the maximum power mixture has been achieved.

If the mixture is set to give a tachometer reading 25 - 50 rpm less than peak rpm on the 'lean' side, the best economy mixture has been achieved. This setting is the one that many aircraft manufacturers recommend (25-50 RPM on the 'lean side' of peak RPM), and their performance claims are based on such a procedure.

Using a mixture that is too lean is a false economy, and will lead to serious engine damage sooner or later. Detonation (an uncontrolled explosive combustion of the mixture in the cylinder) is particularly dangerous, and can lead to an engine failure in a very short time. The use of a fully rich mixture during full power operations is specifically to ensure engine cooling and guard against detonation.

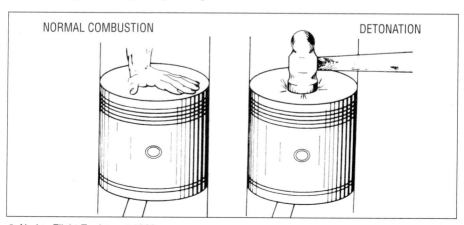

NORMAL COMBUSTION   DETONATION

For any change in operating conditions (altitude, power setting) the mixture will need to be reset. It is particularly important that the mixture is set to fully rich before increasing the power setting.

During a descent from a high altitude, the mixture will gradually become too lean if not reset, leading to excessive cylinder temperatures, power loss and ultimately engine failure. Normally the mixture is set to fully rich prior to landing, unless operating at a high elevation airfield.

Moving the mixture to the fully lean position - ICO (Idle Cut Off) - closes the needle valve and so stops fuel supply to the main metering jet. This is the normal method for closing down the engine and ensures that no unburnt mixture is left in the engine.

The Cessna 172

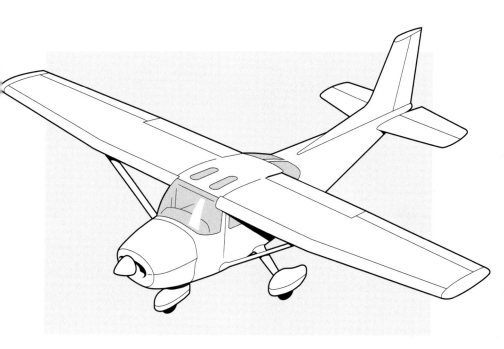

Pre-Flight

Expanded C172 Pre Flight Checklist

Approaching Aircraft

Check for and remove any tie downs, external control locks, pitot cover and wheel chocks.

Look for any oil & fuel spillages from aircraft.

Remove any ice & frost from ALL surfaces.

Check for access to taxiways, obstructions, loose gravel etc.

Look to see if aircraft is on a level surface. Sloping ground will effect the visual check of fuel contents.

In Cabin

1. **Internal Control Locks & Covers** .... Remove and stow securely.
2. **Magneto Switches** .... Check OFF and key out.
3. **Parking Brake** .... Ensure parking brake is set.
4. **Control Wheel Lock** .... Remove and stow.
5. **Master Switch** .... On.

    Turn on Pitot heater, anti-collision beacon, landing lights and navigation lights. Leave cockpit and check in turn :

6. **Pitot Heat** .... Check with fingers that pitot head is warm
    (it may take a minute or so to warm up).

7. **Anti-Collision Beacon** .... Check operation of rotating tail light.

8. **Landing/Nav lights** .... Check.

    For Navigation lights colours are :
    PORT(Left) - RED; STARBOARD(Right) - GREEN; REAR(Tail) - WHITE

    Return to cockpit and turn off electrical services as in above

9. **Fuel** .... Turn on - check contents gauges.
10. **Flaps** .... Check nobody is standing under flaps. Lower fully (40°/30°).
11. **Master Switch** .... Off.
12. **Trimmer** .... Check position neutral using cockpit indicator.
13. **First Aid Kit** .... In Position, secure.
14. **Fire Extinguisher** .... In position, secure & serviceable (gauge at
    top should be in green arc).

Leave cockpit, mind your head on the lowered flaps!

External

Begin at the rear of the wing. This should also be where you complete your checks.

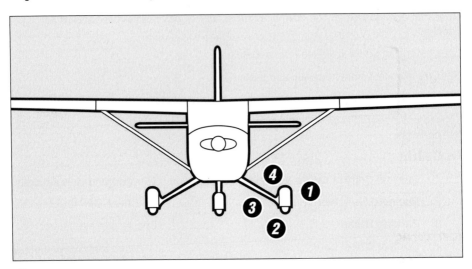

Port Undercarriage

1. **Tyre** .... Check for tread & general condition. Check for correct inflation. Check alignment of creep marks.

2. **Hydraulic Lines** .... Check for leaks (Red fluid).

3. **Disc Brake** .... Should be shiny, not rusty or pitted.

4. **Leg & Fairing** .... Check condition esp. GRP fairing. Look for mud or stone damage on wing & flap surface above or behind undercarriage.

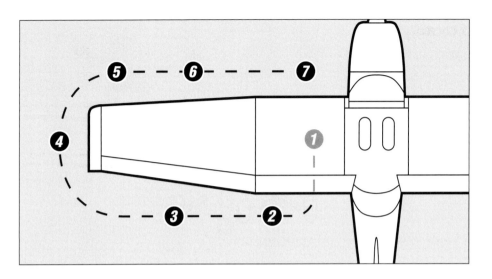

Port Wing

1 **Strut** .... Check condition and security of strut and fairing.

2. **Flap** .... Upper and lower surface condition. Particularly check inner lower surface for mud or stone damage from wheels. Check linkages and runners secure and greased

3. **Aileron** .... Upper and lower surface condition. Linkages & hinges secure, balance weight (lower inside edge) secure (with fingers inside hinge line hold the aileron still with other hand - sudden down movement of aileron makes efficient cutting action!) Check full and free movement - DO NOT USE FORCE.

4. **Wing Tip** .... Condition, security. Navigation lights unbroken. (This area is particularly vulnerable to hangar damage)

5. **Lower Wing Surface** .... Check surface condition.

6. **Wing Leading Edge** .... Check for dents along entire length. Check stall warner. Check pitot head perforations unblocked - DO NOT BLOW INTO PITOT. Check fuel tank vent unblocked.

7. **Fuel Tank** .... CHECK FUEL CONTENTS VISUALLY. Resecure cap. Check upper wing surface condition. Take fuel drain sample from under tank if necessary - check for correct colour, water bubbles or sediment. Check drain not leaking.

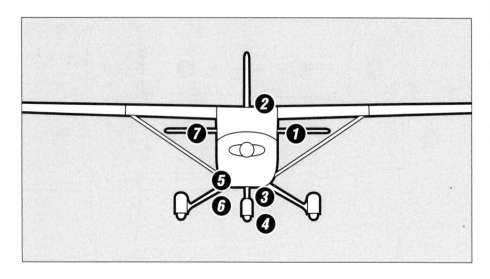

Front Fuselage & Engine

1. **Port Cowling** .... Check general condition and security. Check static vent clear - DO NOT BLOW INTO VENT.

2. **Windscreen** .... Should be clean and insect free.

3. **Nose Leg** .... Oleo extension. Linkages, nuts & split pins secure. No leakage from shimmy damper or oleo.

4. **Nose Wheel** .... Check for tread & general condition. Check for correct inflation. Check alignment of creep marks.

5. **Front Cowling** .... Check condition & security. Intakes clear. Landing lights unbroken.

6. **Propeller** .... Look for cracks or chips especially along the leading edge. Check spinner secure and condition good. DO NOT MOVE OR SWING PROPELLER.

7. **Starboard Cowling** .... Open access flap, check oil level Do NOT overtighten dipstick on resecuring. Operate fuel strainer, if applicable, into a fuel tester. Check fuel strainer closed and not leaking. Check access flap properly closed, cowling secure and good condition.

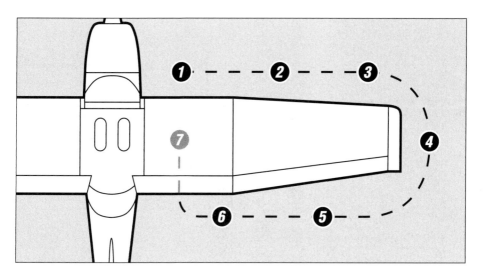

Starboard Wing

1. **Fuel Tank** .... CHECK FUEL CONTENTS VISUALLY. Resecure cap. Whilst at cap check wing upper surface. Take fuel drain sample if necessary from under wing. Check drain not leaking.

2. **Wing Leading Edge** .... Check for dents along entire length.

3. **Lower Wing Surface** .... Check surface condition.

4. **Wing Tip** .... Condition, security. Navigation lights unbroken.

5. **Aileron** .... Upper and lower surface condition, linkages & hinges secure, balance weight (lower inside edge) secure. Remember to watch for aileron movement whilst checking inside hinge line. Check full and free movement gently - DO NOT USE FORCE.

6. **Flap** .... Upper and lower surface condition especially above and behind undercarriage. Check linkages and runners secure and greased.

7. **Strut** .... Condition and security of strut and fairings.

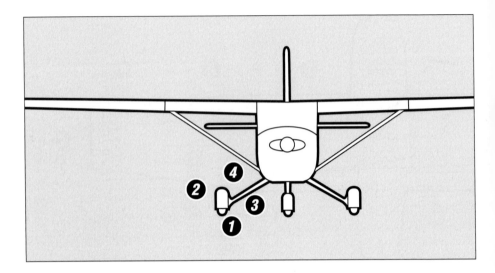

Starboard Undercarriage

1. **Tyre** .... Check for tread & general condition.
   Check for correct inflation. Check alignment of creep marks.

2. **Hydraulic Lines** .... Check for leaks (Red fluid).

3. **Disc Brake** .... Should be shiny, not rusty or pitted.
   Look for mud or stone damage on wing & flap surface near undercarriage.

4. **Leg & Fairing** .... Check condition esp. GRP fairing.
   Look for mud or stone damage on wing & flap surface above or behind
   undercarriage.

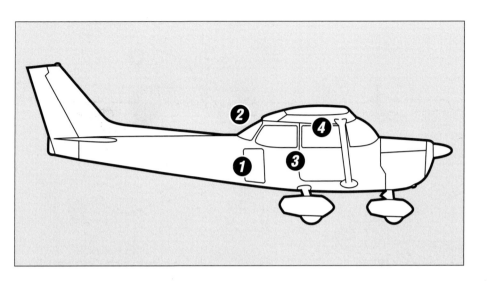

Starboard Fuselage

1. **Skin** .... General surface condition upper and lower, check for wrinkles, dents or punctures.

2. **Radio Aerials** .... Check secure.

3. **Cockpit Door** .... Latches and hinges secure.

4. **Windows** .... Check clean.

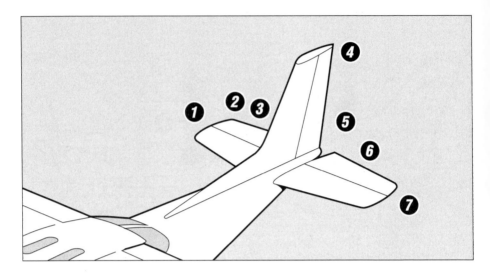

Tail Unit

1 **Starboard Tailplane** .... Check upper and lower surface condition, check security.

2 **Starboard Elevator** .... Check upper and lower surface condition. Check linkages, gently check full and free movement. DO NOT USE FORCE.

3 **Trim Tab** .... Check condition, linkages and correct movement in relation to elevator.

4 **Tail Fin** .... Check condition, also fairings, aerials and rotating beacon.

5 **Rudder** .... Check condition, navigation light, nuts and split pins. Full and free movement - DO NOT USE FORCE. Check tail tie down.

6 **Port Elevator** .... Check condition, check linkages, gently check full and free movement - DO NOT USE FORCE.

7 **Port Tailplane** .... Check condition and security.

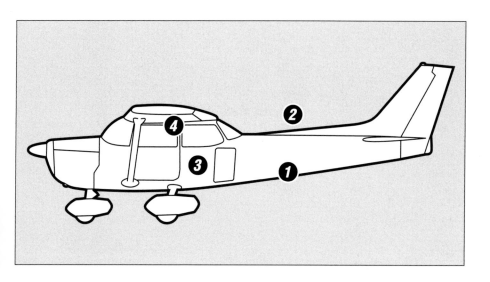

Port Fuselage

1. **Skin** .... General surface condition, upper and lower, look for any wrinkles, dents or punctures.

2. **Radio Aerials** .... Check secure.

3. **Doors** .... Check latches & hinges. Ensure baggage door is secure.

4. **Windows** .... Check clean.

IMPORTANT

REMEMBER: FULL REFERENCE MUST BE MADE TO AIRCRAFT FLIGHT MANUAL, PILOTS OPERATING HANDBOOK, AIP's, FLYING SCHOOL SYLLABUS/PILOTS ORDER BOOK, ETC

IF IN DOUBT - ASK

The Cessna 172

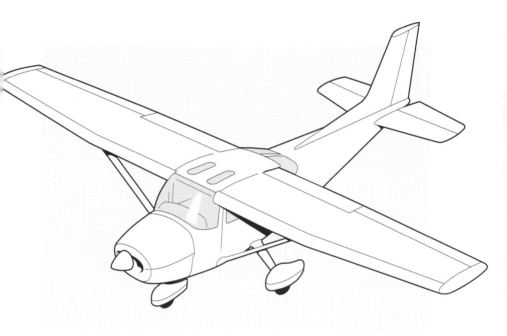

C172 Loading and Performance

Loading

Aircraft loading can be divided into two areas, the aircraft weight and the centre of gravity (c.g.) position.

The aircraft must be loaded so that its weight is below the certified maximum take off weight (2300 lbs/1043 kg for the 172N) or (2400 lbs/1089 kg for the 172P). The flight manual may also list a 'ramp weight', which is the maximum permissible weight for taxying prior to take off. The difference between this and the maximum take off weight allows for the fuel used in taxying and power checks. The weight limit is set primarily as a function of the lifting capability of the aircraft, which is largely determined by the wing design and engine power of the aircraft. Operating the aircraft when it is over weight will adversely affect the aircraft handling and performance, such as:

Increased take off speed and slower acceleration

Increased runway length required for take off

Reduced rate of climb

Reduced maximum altitude capability

Reduced range and endurance

Reduction in manoeuvrability and controllability

Increased stall speed

Increased approach and landing speed

Increased runway length required for landing

The aircraft must also be loaded to ensure that its centre of gravity (c.g.) is within set limits, normally defined as a forward and aft limit aft of the datum, for this aircraft the datum is the lower forward face of the firewall. The forward c.g. limit is determined by the amount of elevator control available at landing speed, the aft c.g. limit is determined by the stability and controllability of the aircraft whilst manoeuvring. Attempted flight with the c.g. position outside the set limits (either forward or aft) will lead to control difficulties, and quite possibly loss of control of the aircraft.

When loading the aircraft it is standard practice to calculate the weight and c.g. position of the aircraft at the same time, commonly known as the weight and balance calculation. Before going further it must be emphasised that the following examples are provided for illustrative purposes only. Each INDIVIDUAL aircraft has an INDIVIDUAL weight schedule that is valid only for that aircraft, and is dependent amongst other things on the equipment fitted to the aircraft. If the aircraft has any major modification, repair or new equipment fitted a new weight schedule will be produced. Therefore for any loading or performance calculations you must use the documents for the specific aircraft you will be using.

As well as setting out limits the aircraft documents will also give lever arms for each item of loading. The lever arm is the distance from the aircraft datum to the item.

The weight multiplied by its lever arm gives its moment. Thus a set weight will have a greater moment the further away from the datum it is.

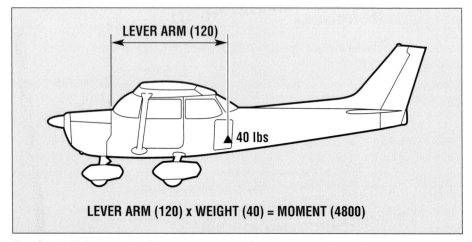

LEVER ARM (120)

▲ 40 lbs

LEVER ARM (120) x WEIGHT (40) = MOMENT (4800)

The C-172 flight manual will include a centre of gravity moment envelope graph, where the weight can be plotted against the total moment.

It is obviously important for the pilot to be sure whether the aircraft needs to operated in the NORMAL or UTILITY category. The aircraft flight manual will advise that certain manoeuvres can only be carried out when the aircraft is loaded within the UTILITY category. Operation in the UTILITY category is defined as a reduced weight (2006lbs/ 910 kg for the 172N; 2100 lbs/953 kg for the 172P) and different c.g. limits. Additionally baggage in the rear baggage area and rear seat passengers are not permitted.

The following examples are done using metres and kg and are based on a C-172N with a maximum take-off weight of 1043kg/2300lbs. Check carefully what limits apply to the aircraft for which you are doing a loading calculation operationally. C-172P models have a higher permitted weight - this information will be found in the aircraft's flight manual and its weight schedule.

The operating weight of the aircraft can be split into three categories:

STANDARD (EMPTY) WEIGHT - the weight of the aircraft, including unusable fuel (and normally full oil). The weight and c.g. position of the aircraft in this condition will be noted in the weight schedule.

VARIABLE LOAD - weight of the crew (ie pilot). The certified minimum crew for this aircraft is one pilot (!). The weight schedule will give the lever arm for this load.

DISPOSABLE LOAD - weight of passengers, fuel and baggage. Again the weight schedule will give a lever arm for each of these loads.

Firstly the pilot will need to calculate a weight for the variable and disposable load. It is obviously important to work in one set of units (either lbs or kgs). This becomes more complicated for the fuel load where volume (litres, imperial gallons or U S gallons) will need to be converted into weight. This may be done in the weight schedule, but conversion tables are set out in section 7.

Weight And Centre Of Gravity Schedule

PRODUCED BY :

GROSVENOR AVIATION SERVICES (ENGINEERING) LIMITED

AIRCRAFT TYPE: PIPER PA38-112

NATIONALITY AND REGISTRATION MARKS: G-BGRR

CONSTRUCTOR'S SERIAL No: 78A0336

MAXIMUM PERMISSIBLE WEIGHT: 1670 lbs

MAXIMUM LANDING WEIGHT: 1670 lbs

CENTRE OF GRAVITY LIMITS: REFER TO FLIGHT MANUAL REP No. FAA 2126

ALL LEVER ARMS ARE DISTANCES IN INCHES EITHER FORE OR AFT OF DATUM.

PART 'A' BASIC WEIGHT

The basic weight of this aircraft as calculated from Planeweighs Limited Report No.1034 weighed on 08.07.88. at Manchester Airport is: **1182 lbs**

The centre of gravity of aircraft in the same condition (aft of the datum) is: **74.66 ins**.

The total Moment about the datum in this condition in lb ins. is: **88254.45**

The DATUM referred to is defined in the Flight Manual, which is **66.25 ins**. forward of Wing leading edge.

The basic weight includes the weight of 12 lbs unuseable fuel and 45 lbs of oil and the weight of items indicated in Appendix 1 which comprises the list of basic equipment carried.

Each individual aircraft has an individual weight schedule, valid only for that aircraft. The weight schedule will state lever arms for each item of loading.

Mathematical Weight and Balance Calculation

With this method of calculation the weights of each item are listed together with their lever arm. Addition of all the weights is the first step, to ensure that the resulting figure is within the maximum permitted. Assuming this is the case the balance can then be calculated. For each item (except the basic weight where the moment calculation is already done on the weight schedule) the weight is multiplied by the lever arm, to give the moment. Normally the lever arm is aft of the datum, to give a positive figure. If the lever arm quoted is forward of the datum and resulting lever arm the moment will be negative (although obviously the weight is NOT deducted from the weight calculation). All the moments are added together, to give the total moment, and this figure is then divided by the total weight. The resulting figure will be the position of the centre of gravity, which can be checked to ensure it is within the set limits. The weight and c.g. position can be plotted on a graph in the flight manual. If the plotted position is within the 'envelope', the weight and c.g. position are within limits.

EXAMPLE

BASIC (EMPTY) WEIGHT: C-172N G-AAAA
From the weight schedule for this aircraft,
the weight is 654.7 kg.

VARIABLE LOAD: Pilot 75 kg

DISPOSABLE LOAD: Co-Pilot 70kg
Full Usable Fuel (40 US gal) 109kg
1 X Rear seat passenger 70kg
Baggage Area 1 14 kg
Baggage Area 2   10kg

These figures are put into a table to check weight and balance. Remember the moment is calculated by multiplying item weight by item lever arm. The lever arm is given in the weight schedule and flight manual.

ITEM	WEIGHT (kg)	LEVER ARM (m)	MOMENT (kg/m)
BASIC (EMPTY) WEIGHT - the basic weight and its moment is given in the weight schedule.			
G-AAAA	654.7	0.97	638.57
VARIABLE LOAD			
Pilot	75	0.94	70.5
DISPOSABLE LOAD			
Co-Pilot	70	0.94	65.8
Fuel	109	1.15	125.35
1 X Rear Seat Passenger	70	1.85	129.5
Baggage Area 1	14	2.41	33.74
Baggage Area 2	10	3.12	31.20
TOTAL WEIGHT 1002.70		TOTAL MOMENT 1094.66	

The total weight is below the maximum permitted (1043kg) and so is acceptable. If the total moment is divided by the total weight - the result is the c.g. position (in metres aft of the datum).

$$\frac{1094.66}{1002.70} = 1.09 \text{ metres (aft of datum)}.$$

The flight manual contains a graph where total weight can be plotted against TOTAL moment (and so save the calculation of dividing the total moment by total weight). When the total weight and total moment are plotted on this graph, the aircraft is seen to be loaded within the NORMAL category. Operation in the NORMAL category does mean that certain manoeuvres are prohibited and the permitted 'G' limits are reduced.

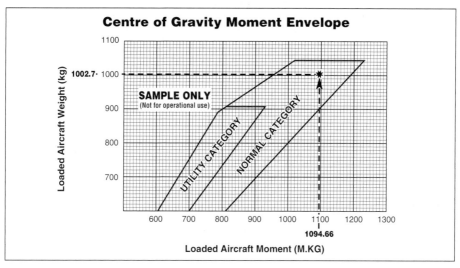

Should the pilot wish to perform one of the manoeuvres restricted to operating the aircraft in the UTILITY category, it is firstly necessary (before flight!) to remove the rear seat passenger(s) and any rear baggage. Assuming the other items remain the same, the same table can be re-calculated.

ITEM	WEIGHT (kg)	LEVER ARM (m)	MOMENT
BASIC (Empty) WEIGHT			
G-AAAA C-172N	654.7	0.97	638.57
VARIABLE LOAD			
Pilot	75	0.94	70.5
DISPOSABLE LOAD			
Co-Pilot	70	0.94	65.8
Fuel	109	1.15	125.35
	908.7		900.22

We can see that the total weight is now below the maximum permitted for UTILITY operations (910 kg for C-172N) and so is acceptable. Total moment can be divided by total weight to give the c.g. position:

$$\frac{900.22}{908.70} = 0.99M \text{ aft of datum}$$

The total weight can be plotted against the total moment on the centre of gravity moment envelope graph:

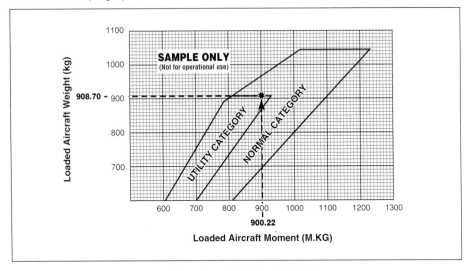

It can be seen that the aircraft IS loaded within the UTILITY category.

Use of the Loading Graph

The flight manual will contain a loading graph that can be used to simplify the weight and balance calculation. It does this by allowing the pilot to find the moment for each item weight without even needing to know the lever arm (useful if you've forgotten your calculator). Using the figures from the first example, the loading graph can be used like this:

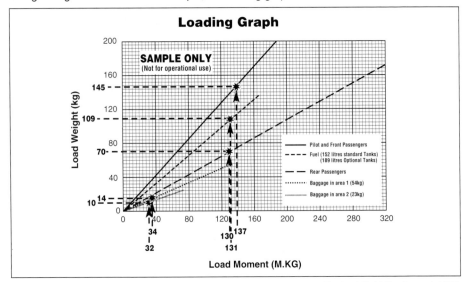

The resulting figures go into a simplified table:

ITEM	WEIGHT (kg)	MOMENT
G-AAAA (from the weight schedule)	654.7	638.57
Pilot / Co-Pilot	145	137
Fuel	109	131
1 X Rear Seat Passenger	70	130
Baggage Area 1	14	34
Baggage Area 2	10	32
	1002.7	1102.57

Again total moment can be divided by total weight:

$$\frac{1102.57}{1002.70} = 1.10\text{m aft of datum}$$

These figures can be plotted on the centre of gravity moment envelope to check the loading.

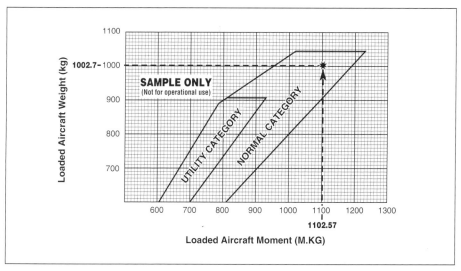

Loaded Aircraft Moment (M.KG)

Using the loading graph has given a slightly different c.g. position to that obtained from the mathematical calculation. If the c.g position is very close to the c.g. limits, the mathematical calculation will always give the most accurate answer.

The C-172 is often described as an aircraft in which you can fill all the seats, the baggage area and the fuel tanks and just get airborne. In fact this is not necessarily the case. If you re-do the above calculation, but add an extra adult rear-seat passenger and an extra 30kg of baggage, you will find the weight exceeds the maximum permitted for a C-172N (1043 kg) by some kgs. Something from the disposable load will have to go - and as the Pilot in Command it is your decision what to leave behind!

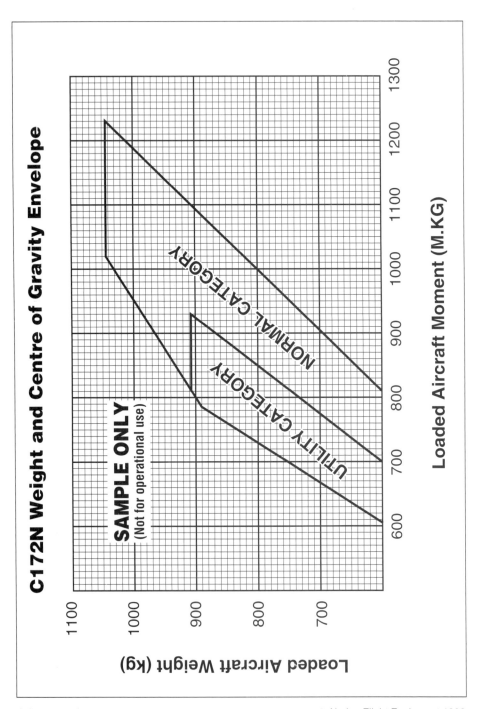

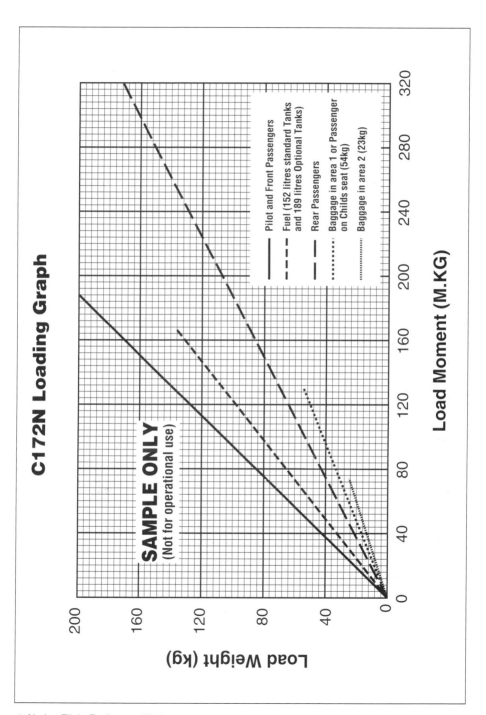

> **A WORD OF WARNING**. As well as the safety aspect, operating the aircraft outside its weight and balance envelope has far-reaching legal and financial implications. Almost the first thing an accident investigator will check after an accident is the loading of the aircraft. If the loading is outside limits the pilot is contravening the Air Navigation Order. In addition both the aircraft's insurance company and the pilot's personal insurance company will be unsympathetic when they know that the conditions of the Certificate of Airworthiness (ie the flight manual limitations) were not complied with. As the pilot in command you are responsible.

Performance

The aircraft's flight manual contains a section of tables and graphs to allow the pilot to calculate the expected performance of the aircraft for different flight phases. Undoubtedly the most commonly used tables are those for take off and landing performance, and those are the ones we will concentrate on here, however the same principles can be used on the other tables. Two things to remember: firstly the flight manual performance is obtained by using the recommended techniques - to get table results follow table procedures. Secondly you can safely assume that the flight manual results have been obtained by placing a brand new aircraft in the hands of an experienced test pilot flying under favourable conditions. To make allowances for a less than new aircraft, being flown by an average mortal in the real world it is wise to 'factor' any results you get. This may be done in the flight manual, but if not some form of safety factoring is highly recommended. Public transport operations are subject to any overall factoring of 1.33 for take offs and 1.43 for landings, this figure being incorporated in the relevant graphs. It is highly recommended that the pilot apply the same factor to any table figures ie a calculated take off distance of 500 metres becomes 500 X 1.33 = 665 metres. As with loading calculations the pilot must use the tables and data from the documents for the individual aircraft being used. The tables and diagrams used in this section are for illustrative purposes only, and not for operational use.

Section 7 contains recommended factors for variations not necessarily covered in the flight manual, as well as conversion factors between feet and metres; lbs and kgs; °C and °F etc.

C-172 Take-off and Landing Performance Tables

The take-off and landing distance tables in the flight manual make several assumptions (eg paved, level, dry runway; use of flight manual technique etc). The concept of these tables is that they actually show the resulting performance figure (eg take-off distance, landing distance etc) for a particular set of parameters (eg aircraft weight, pressure altitude, temperature). As the conditions for the flight you are planning are unlikely to fit exactly into those given on the performance tables it will be necessary to 'average' between parameters above and below your actual conditions.

Depending on the model year and country of manufacture the table distances may be given in feet or metres. In addition the temperature may be in °C or °F, speeds in knots, mph, or kph, weight in lbs or kg, or any combination of these! This can be a recipe for confusion, so check the flight manual carefully to be sure what units you are using. Always apply a common sense check - if the results you are getting look more appropriate to a microlight (or a 747) there may be a mistake; if in doubt - check.

The tables use the term "Pressure Altitude". This is the altitude of the runway assuming standard pressure setting (ie 1013 mb - or 1013 hPa if you prefer). When the QNH is other than 1013 you will need to adjust the actual altitude to get the pressure altitude. At the aircraft this can be done by simply setting the altimeter to 1013 and taking the indicated altitude. Without an altimeter handy, adjust the actual altitude by 30' for each millibar/hectopascal above or below 1013. Remember when the QNH is above 1013 the pressure altitude is less than actual, and vice versa.

The headwind or tailwind component is calculated from the windspeed and angle of wind direction to the runway. (eg a 10 knot wind directly down the runway gives a headwind component of 10 knots; a 10 knot wind at 90° gives a headwind component of zero. There is a graph in section 7 for calculation of head/tailwind component and crosswind component.

The take-off and landing distance tables will contain a reminder to check the flight manual recommended technique. To get the flight manual results you must use the flight manual technique.

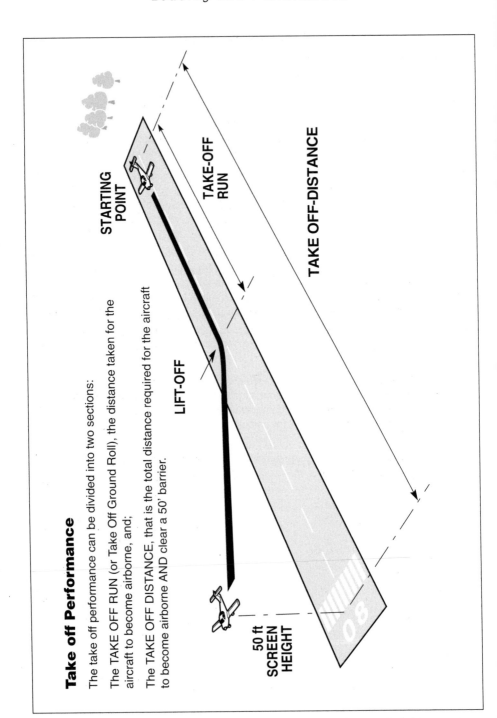

Take off Performance

The take off performance can be divided into two sections:

The TAKE OFF RUN (or Take Off Ground Roll), the distance taken for the aircraft to become airborne, and;

The TAKE OFF DISTANCE, that is the total distance required for the aircraft to become airborne AND clear a 50' barrier.

STARTING POINT

TAKE-OFF RUN

TAKE OFF-DISTANCE

LIFT-OFF

50 ft SCREEN HEIGHT

Take-off Distance Calculation Example

For this example we will take the conditions as:
Outside air temperature +12°C
Pressure altitude 740ft
Zero Wind
Take-Off weight 2200lbs/998 kg

Firstly go to the table for max. gross weight (1043 kg for a C-172N). The temperature is rounded UP to +15°C and the pressure altitude is rounded UP to 1000'.

						0°C / 32°F		10°C / 50°F		20°C / 68°F		30°C / 86°F		40°C
TAKE OFF DISTANCE									**SHORT FIELD**					
CONDITIONS :		Flaps up		Full throttle prior to brake release					Paved, Level, Dry runway					Zero w
MAXIMUM WEIGHT	IAS		PRESSURE ALTITUDE			0°C / 32°F		10°C / 50°F		20°C / 68°F		30°C / 86°F		40°C
	LIFT OFF	AT 15M (50ft)	FT	M		GROUND ROLL M	TOTAL TO CLEAR 15M OBS. M	GROUND ROLL M	TOTAL TO CLEAR 15M OBS. M	GROUND ROLL M	TOTAL TO CLEAR 15M OBS. M	GROUND ROLL M	TOTAL TO CLEAR 15M OBS. M	GROUND ROLL M
1043kg	96km/h	109km/h	Sea Level			219	396	236	424	255	454	273	485	293
	52kt	59kt	1000	305		241	433	259	465	279	497	299	532	320

Along the 1000' line, average between the figure given for +20°C (497m) and that given for +10°C (465m). The quickest way to do this averaging is to add the two figures together and divide by two, so;

$$465 + 497 = 962, \quad 962 \div 2 = 481m$$

This process is now repeated using the next table down in weight (953 kg). Averaging between the +10°C and +20°C parameters at 1000' pressure altitude gives a figure of 392m.

						0°C / 32°F		10°C / 50°F		20°C / 68°F		30°C / 86°F		40°C
TAKE OFF DISTANCE									**SHORT FIELD**					
CONDITIONS :		Flaps up		Full throttle prior to brake release					Paved, Level, Dry runway					Zero w
MAXIMUM WEIGHT	IAS		PRESSURE ALTITUDE			0°C / 32°F		10°C / 50°F		20°C / 68°F		30°C / 86°F		40°C
	LIFT OFF	AT 15M (50ft)	FT	M		GROUND ROLL M	TOTAL TO CLEAR 15M OBS. M	GROUND ROLL M	TOTAL TO CLEAR 15M OBS. M	GROUND ROLL M	TOTAL TO CLEAR 15M OBS. M	GROUND ROLL M	TOTAL TO CLEAR 15M OBS. M	GROUND ROLL M
953kg	93km/h	104km/h	Sea Level			178	326	192	347	207	372	221	396	238
	50kt	56kt	1000	305		195	355	210	379	226	405	242	433	259

By sheer coincidence (!) the actual take-off weight of 998 kg falls exactly halfway between the table weights of 1043kg and 953kg. Therefore we can take a straight average between the two calculated figures;

$$481 + 392 = 873; \quad 873 \div 2 = 436.5m \text{ - say } 437m.$$

This figure is now multiplied by the take off safety factor of 1.33;

$$437 \times 1.33 = 581m$$

In part the safety factor will help cover over any errors that may have occurred in the averaging process.

6.*13*

Landing Performance

The landing performance is calculated as the LANDING DISTANCE, that is the total distance from 50' over the runway to a full stop. The ground roll (or ground run) - the distance from touch down to full stop-may also be calculated.

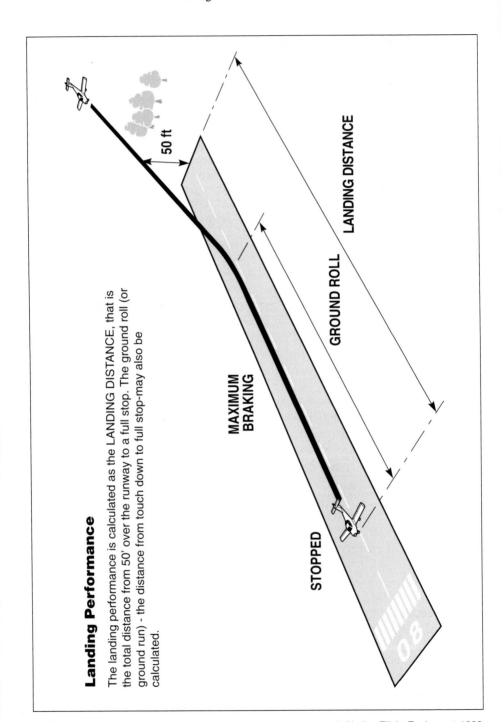

50 ft

MAXIMUM
BRAKING

STOPPED

GROUND ROLL

LANDING DISTANCE

08

Landing Distance Example

Weight 2200 lbs (998 kg)
Outside air temperature +12°C
Pressure Altitude 1240'
Headwind component 5 knots
Level runway, short wet grass

To calculate landing distance just one chart is given in the flight manual - for landing at the max. gross weight (for a C-172N) of 1043kg. Although strictly speaking landing distance does decrease with reduced weight, it is best to use the table figures and accept that when landing at a lower weight you will have a greater safety margin over the 'book' figure. Also to simplify the calculation the pressure altitude is rounded UP to 1500', and the temperature is rounded UP to +15°C.

Firstly take the figures at +10°C and +20°C along the 1000' line (386m & 396m). The average between these figures is 391m. This process is now repeated along the 2000' pressure altitude line, to obtain an average of 402m (to the nearest metre).

		LANDING DISTANCE		SHORT FIELD							
CONDITIONS :		Flaps 40°		Power off		Maximum braking		Paved, Level, Dry runway			
WEIGHT	IAS	PRESSURE ALTITUDE		0°C / 32°F		10°C / 50°F		20°C / 68°F		30°C / 86°F	
	At 15M (50ft)	FT	M	GROUND ROLL M	TOTAL TO CLEAR 15M OBS. M	GROUND ROLL M	TOTAL TO CLEAR 15M OBS. M	GROUND ROLL M	TOTAL TO CLEAR 15M OBS. M	GROUND ROLL M	TOTAL TO CLEAR 15M OBS. M
1043kg	111km/h	Sea Level		151	367	155	376	162	386	166	395
	60kt	1000	305	155	376	162	386	168	396	172	405
	69mph	2000	610	162	386	168	396	174	407	180	418

When these two figures are averaged we get a 'base-line' figure;

$$391 + 402 = 793; 793 \div 2 = 397m$$

This base-line figure is now factored to allow for the headwind. The table states that landing distance is reduced by 10% for each 9 knots of headwind, so for 5 knots of headwind:

$$5 \div 9 \times 10\% = 5.5\%$$

When 397m is reduced by 5.5% (397 X 0.945), the landing distance becomes 375m. To allow for the runway surface (short wet grass), this figure is now multiplied by the factor given in section 7 (page 7.2):

$$375m \times 1.3 = 488m$$

Finally, this figure is multiplied by the landing safety factor (1.43) to get the landing distance required:

$$488m \times 1.43 = 698m - \text{this is our final figure.}$$

Obviously all this averaging can get tedious, and you may need a calculator. An alternative is just to 'round-up' the data you have to the next pressure altitude/temperature shown on the table. If you do this using the conditions as before, the final figure becomes 757m - an extra 59m. You might think this is not a great difference for a much quicker calculation.

C172N Take-off Distances – Short field (1043kg)

TAKE OFF DISTANCE — SHORT FIELD

CONDITIONS: Flaps up / Full throttle prior to brake release / Paved, Level, Dry runway / Zero wind

IAS — LIFT OFF: 96km/h, 52kt, 60mph — AT 15M (50ft): 109km/h, 59kt, 68mph

MAXIMUM WEIGHT: 1043kg

PRESSURE ALTITUDE FT	PRESSURE ALTITUDE M	0°C / 32°F GROUND ROLL M	0°C / 32°F TOTAL TO CLEAR 15M OBS. M	10°C / 50°F GROUND ROLL M	10°C / 50°F TOTAL TO CLEAR 15M OBS. M	20°C / 68°F GROUND ROLL M	20°C / 68°F TOTAL TO CLEAR 15M OBS. M	30°C / 86°F GROUND ROLL M	30°C / 86°F TOTAL TO CLEAR 15M OBS. M	40°C / 104°F GROUND ROLL M	40°C / 104°F TOTAL TO CLEAR 15M OBS. M
Sea Level		219	396	236	424	255	454	273	485	293	518
1000	305	241	433	259	465	279	497	299	532	320	568
2000	610	264	474	283	509	305	546	328	584	352	626
3000	914	290	521	312	559	335	600	361	645	387	690
4000	1219	319	573	353	617	369	663	396	712	427	765
5000	1524	351	632	378	683	407	735	437	791	469	852
6000	1829	386	703	416	757	450	817	483	882	520	953
7000	2134	427	782	460	844	497	914	535	989	576	1071
8000	2438	472	875	511	948	550	1029	593	1119	639	1216

C172N Take-off Distances – Short field (953kg)

TAKE OFF DISTANCE – SHORT FIELD

CONDITIONS:
- Flaps up
- Full throttle prior to brake release
- Paved, Level, Dry runway
- Zero wind

IAS		MAXIMUM WEIGHT	PRESSURE ALTITUDE		0°C / 32°F		10°C / 50°F		20°C / 68°F		30°C / 86°F		40°C / 104°F	
LIFT OFF	AT 15M (50ft)		FT	M	GROUND ROLL M	TOTAL TO CLEAR 15M OBS. M	GROUND ROLL M	TOTAL TO CLEAR 15M OBS. M	GROUND ROLL M	TOTAL TO CLEAR 15M OBS. M	GROUND ROLL M	TOTAL TO CLEAR 15M OBS. M	GROUND ROLL M	TOTAL TO CLEAR 15M OBS. M
93km/h	104km/h	**953kg**	Sea Level		178	326	192	347	207	372	221	396	238	424
50kt	56kt		1000	305	195	355	210	379	226	405	242	433	259	463
58mph	64mph		2000	610	213	381	230	415	247	443	265	474	285	507
			3000	914	335	424	253	454	271	486	291	521	312	558
			4000	1219	258	465	287	500	299	535	320	573	344	614
			5000	1524	283	512	305	550	328	590	352	632	378	680
			6000	1829	312	564	335	607	361	652	389	701	418	754
			7000	2134	344	625	370	674	399	725	430	780	462	840
			8000	2438	379	693	410	750	442	809	475	873	512	942

C172N Landing Distances – Short field

LANDING DISTANCE SHORT FIELD

CONDITIONS: Flaps 40°, Power off, Maximum braking, Paved, Level, Dry runway, Zero wind

IAS At 15M (50ft): 111km/h, 60kt, 69mph

WEIGHT: 1043kg

PRESSURE ALTITUDE		0°C / 32°F		10°C / 50°F		20°C / 68°F		30°C / 86°F		40°C / 104°F	
FT	M	GROUND ROLL M	TOTAL TO CLEAR 15M OBS. M	GROUND ROLL M	TOTAL TO CLEAR 15M OBS. M	GROUND ROLL M	TOTAL TO CLEAR 15M OBS. M	GROUND ROLL M	TOTAL TO CLEAR 15M OBS. M	GROUND ROLL M	TOTAL TO CLEAR 15M OBS. M
Sea Level		151	367	155	376	162	386	166	395	172	405
1000	305	155	376	162	386	168	396	172	405	178	416
2000	610	162	386	168	396	174	407	180	418	186	428
3000	914	168	396	174	407	180	418	186	428	192	439
4000	1219	174	407	183	418	187	430	194	440	200	451
5000	1524	180	418	187	431	194	442	200	453	207	465
6000	1829	187	431	195	443	201	454	209	468	215	479
7000	2134	195	443	201	456	209	468	216	480	223	492
8000	2438	203	457	210	469	216	482	224	494	232	507

Cruise Performance

The cruise performance tables can be used in the same way as the take-off and landing distance tables.

The cruise performance tables use the concept of a 'standard temperature' at altitude, based on the International Standard Atmosphere conditions of +15°C temperature at sea level, and a lapse rate of 1.98°C per 1000'. To help in using the cruise performance tables, the 'Standard Temperatures' for given altitudes are listed below:

2000'	+11°C
4000'	+7°C
6000'	+3°C
8000'	-1°C
10000'	-5°C
12000'	-9°C

It is wise to factor any cruise performance figures calculated by deducting at least 10% from performance (eg increase calculated fuel consumption by 10%), and remember the figures assume the use of the flight manual recommended mixture leaning procedure. If you do not use this procedure the actual fuel consumption could be up to 25% MORE than the table figures, with a resulting reduction in range and endurance. It is necessary to allow a more than adequate fuel margin - say not less than 45 mins fuel reserve on landing. The infinite number of variables that can affect any flight (stronger than forecast headwind, change of routing, higher than expected fuel consumption, excessive holding time prior to take-off etc) make it foolhardy to attempt to fly to the very limit of the calculated range/endurance.

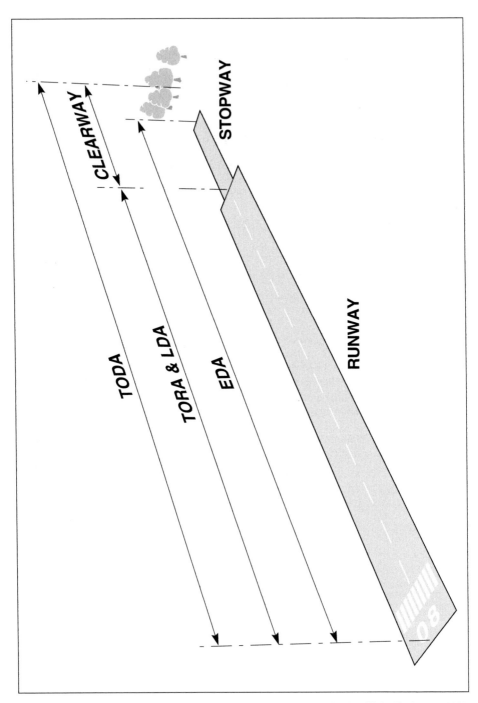

Runway Dimensions

Having calculated the distances the aircraft requires for take off or landing, the runway dimensions must be checked to ensure that the aircraft can be safely operated on the runway in question. The figures given in the AIP or airfield guide can be defined in a number of ways.

The Take Off Run Available (TORA)

The TORA is the length of the runway available for the take off ground run of the aircraft. This is usually the physical length of the runway.

The Emergency Distance (ED)

The ED is the length of the TORA plus the length of any stopway. A stopway is an area at the end of the TORA prepared for an aircraft to stop on in the event of an abandoned take off. The ED is also known as the

ACCELERATE - STOP DISTANCE AVAILABLE.

The Take Off Distance Available (TODA)

The TODA is the TORA plus the length of any clearway. A clearway is an area over which an aircraft may make its initial climb (to 50' in this instance). The TODA will not be more than 1.5 X TORA.

The Landing Distance Available (LDA)

The LDA is the length of the runway available for the ground run of an aircraft landing. In all cases the landing distance required should never be greater than the landing distance available.

The Cessna 172

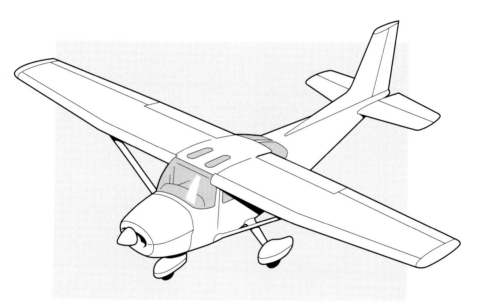

Conversions

Take-off Distance Factors

The following factors will allow the pilot to make allowance for variations that may affect take-off performance. Although some of these factors are covered in the C172 performance tables, the table is produced in its entirety for completeness:

VARIATION	INCREASE IN TAKE-OFF DISTANCE (to 50')	FACTOR
10% increase in aircraft weight	20%	1.2
Increase of 1000' in runway altitude	10%	1.1
Increase in temperature of 10°C	10%	1.1
Dry Grass		
- Short (under 5 inches)	20%	1.2
- Long (5 - 10 inches)	25%	1.25
Wet Grass		
- Short	25%	1.25
- Long	30%	1.3
2% uphill slope	10%	1.1
Tailwind component of 10% of lift off speed	20%	1.2
Soft ground or snow *	at least 25%	at least 1.25

* snow and other runway contamination is covered on page 7.3.

Landing Distance Factors

The following factors will allow the pilot to make allowance for variations that may affect landing performance. Although some of these factors are covered in the C172 performance tables, the table is produced in its entirety for completeness:

VARIATION	INCREASE IN LANDING DISTANCE (from 50')	FACTOR
10% increase in aircraft weight	10%	1.1
Increase of 1000' in runway altitude	5%	1.05
Increase in temperature of 10°C	5%	1.05
Dry Grass		
- Short (under 5 inches)	20%	1.2
- Long (5 - 10 inches)	30%	1.3
Wet Grass		
- Short	30%	1.30
- Long	40%	1.40
2% downhill slope	10%	1.1
Tailwind component of 10% of landing speed	20%	1.2
snow *	at least 25%	at least 1.25

* snow and other runway contamination is covered on page 7.3.

Runway Contamination

A runway can be contaminated by water, snow or slush. If operation on such a runway cannot be avoided additional allowance must be made for the problems such contamination may cause - ie additional drag, reduced braking performance (possible aquaplaning), and directional control problems.

It is generally recommended that take-off should not be attempted if dry snow covers the runway to a depth of more than 60mm, or if water, slush or wet snow covers the runway to more than 15mm. In addition a tailwind, or crosswind component exceeding 10 knots, should not be accepted when operating on a slippery runway.

For take-off distance required calculations the other known conditions should be factored, and the emergency distance available on the runway should be at least 2.0 X the take-off distance required (for a paved runway) or at least 2.66 X the take-off distance required (for a grass runway).

When landing any water or slush can have a very adverse effect on landing performance, and the danger of aquaplaning (with negligible wheel braking and loss of directional control) is very real.

Use of the Wind Component Graph

This graph can be used to find the head/tail wind component and the crosswind component, given a particular wind velocity and runway direction.

EXAMPLE:

> Runway 27
>
> Surface wind 240°/15 knots

The angle between the runway direction (270°) and wind direction(240°) is 30°. Now on the graph locate a point on the 30° line, where it crosses the 15 knot arc. From this point take a horizontal line to give the headwind component (13 knots) and a vertical line to give the crosswind component (8 knots).

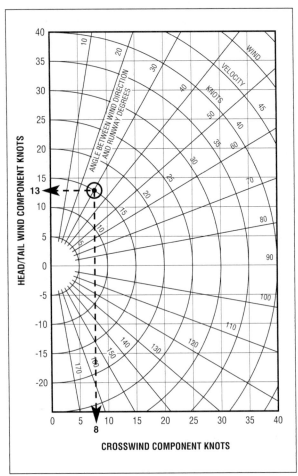

On the main graph overleaf the shaded area represents the maximum demonstrated crosswind component for this aircraft. If the wind point is within this shaded area, the maximum demonstrated crosswind component for this aircraft has been exceeded.

Note: Runway direction will be degrees magnetic. Check the wind direction given is also in degrees magnetic.

Wind Component Graph

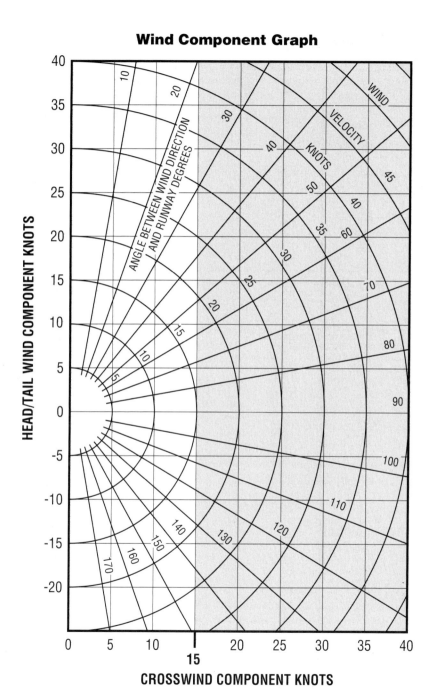

Conversions

TEMPERATURE

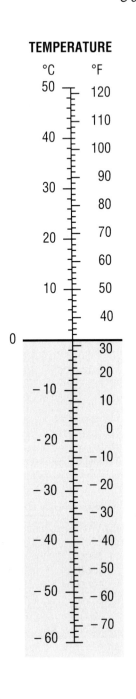

PRESSURE

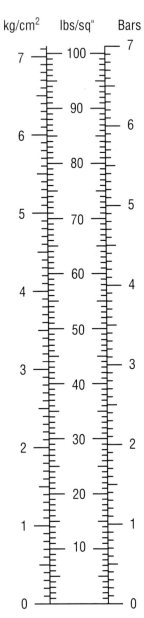

Distance-Metres/Feet

Metres	Feet		Feet	Metres
1	3.28		1	0.30
2	6.56		2	0.61
3	9.84		3	0.91
4	13.12		4	1.22
5	16.40		5	1.52
6	19.69		6	1.83
7	22.97		7	2.13
8	26.25		8	2.44
9	29.53		9	2.74
10	32.81		10	3.05
20	65.62		20	6.10
30	98.43		30	9.14
40	131.23		40	12.19
50	164.04		50	15.24
60	196.85		60	18.29
70	229.66		70	21.34
80	262.47		80	24.38
90	295.28		90	27.43
100	328.08		100	30.48
200	656.16		200	60.96
300	984.25		300	91.44
400	1,312.34		400	121.92
500	1,640.42		500	152.40
600	1,968.50		600	182.88
700	2,296.59		700	213.36
800	2,624.67		800	243.84
900	2,952.76		900	274.32
1000	3,280.84		1000	304.80
2000	6,561.70		2000	609.60
3000	9,842.50		3000	914.40
4000	13.123.40		4000	1,219.20
5000	16,404.20		5000	1,524.00
6000	19,685.00		6000	1,828.80
7000	22,965.90		7000	2,133.60
8000	26,246.70		8000	2,438.40
9000	29,527.60		9000	2,743.20
10000	32,808.40		10000	3,048.00

Conversion Factors:

Centimetres to Inches x .3937
Inches to Centimetres x 2.54

Metres to Feet x 3.28084
Feet to Metres x 0.3048

Distance-KM/Nautical Miles/Statute Miles

NM	Km	St		Km	NM	St		ST	NM	Km
1	1.85	1.15		1	.54	.62		1	.87	1.61
2	3.70	2.30		2	1.08	1.24		2	1.74	3.22
3	5.56	3.45		3	1.62	1.86		3	2.61	4.83
4	7.41	4.60		4	2.16	2.49		4	3.48	6.44
5	9.26	5.75		5	2.70	3.11		5	4.34	8.05
6	11.11	6.90		6	3.24	3.73		6	5.21	9.66
7	12.96	8.06		7	3.78	4.35		7	6.08	11.27
8	14.82	9.21		8	4.32	4.97		8	6.95	12.87
9	16.67	10.36		9	4.86	5.59		9	7.82	14.48
10	18.52	11.51		10	5.40	6.21		10	8.69	16.09
20	37.04	23.02		20	10.80	12.43		20	17.38	32.19
30	55.56	34.52		30	16.20	18.64		30	26.07	48.28
40	74.08	46.03		40	21.60	24.86		40	34.76	64.37
50	92.60	57.54		50	27.00	31.07		50	43.45	80.47
60	111.12	69.05		60	32.40	37.28		60	52.14	96.56
70	129.64	80.55		70	37.80	43.50		70	60.83	112.65
80	148.16	92.06		80	43.20	49.71		80	69.52	128.75
90	166.68	103.57		90	48.60	55.92		90	78.21	144.84
100	185.2	115.1		100	54.0	62.1		100	86.9	161.0
200	370.4	230.2		200	108.0	124.3		200	173.8	321.9
300	555.6	345.2		300	162.0	186.4		300	260.7	482.8
400	740.8	460.3		400	216.0	248.6		400	347.6	643.7
500	926.0	575.4		500	270.0	310.7		500	434.5	804.7
600	1111.2	690.5		600	324.0	372.8		600	521.4	965.6
700	1296.4	805.6		700	378.0	435.0		700	608.3	1126.5
800	1481.6	920.6		800	432.0	497.1		800	695.2	1287.5
900	1666.8	1035.7		900	486.0	559.2		900	782.1	1448.4

Conversion Factors:

Statute Miles to Nautical Miles x 0.868976
Statute Miles to Kilometres x 1.60934
Kilometres to Statute Miles x 0.62137
Kilometres to Nautical Miles x 0.539957
Nautical Miles to Statute Miles x 1.15078
Nautical Miles to Kilometres x 1.852

Weight

lbs	Kg	Kg	lbs
1	.45	1	2.20
2	.91	2	4.41
3	1.38	3	6.61
4	1.81	4	8.82
5	2.27	5	11.02
6	2.72	6	13.23
7	3.18	7	15.43
8	3.63	8	17.64
9	4.08	9	19.84
10	4.54	10	22.05
20	9.07	20	44.09
30	13.61	30	66.14
40	18.14	40	88.18
50	22.68	50	110.23
60	27.22	60	132.28
70	31.75	70	154.32
80	36.29	80	176.37
90	40.82	90	198.42
100	45.4	100	220.5
200	90.7	200	440.9
300	136.1	300	661.4
400	181.4	400	881.8
500	226.8	500	1102.3
600	272.2	600	1322.8
700	317.5	700	1543.2
800	362.9	800	1763.7
900	408.2	900	1984.2
1000	453.6	1000	2204.6
2000	907.2	2000	4409.2
3000	1360.8	3000	6613.9
4000	1814.4	4000	8818.5
5000	2268.0	5000	11023.1
6000	2721.5	6000	13227.7
7000	3175.1	7000	15432.3
8000	3628.7	8000	17637.0
9000	4082.3	9000	19841.6
10000	4535.9	10000	22046.2

Conversion Factors:

lbs to Kilograms x 0.45359
Kilograms to lbs x 2.20462

Volume (Fluid)

Litres	Imp. Gall	U.S. Gall	U.S. Gall	Imp. Gall	Litres	Imp. Gall	U.S. Gall	Litres
1	0.22	0.26	1	0.83	3.79	1	1.20	4.55
2	0.44	0.53	2	1.67	7.57	2	2.40	9.09
3	0.66	0.79	3	2.50	11.36	3	3.60	13.64
4	0.88	1.06	4	3.33	15.14	4	4.80	18.18
5	1.10	1.32	5	4.16	18.93	5	6.00	22.73
6	1.32	1.59	6	5.00	22.71	6	7.21	27.28
7	1.54	1.85	7	5.83	26.50	7	8.41	31.82
8	1.76	2.11	8	6.66	30.28	8	9.61	36.37
9	1.98	2.38	9	7.49	34.07	9	10.81	40.91
10	2.20	2.64	10	8.33	37.85	10	12.01	45.46
20	4.40	5.28	20	16.65	75.71	20	24.02	90.92
30	6.60	7.93	30	24.98	113.56	30	36.03	136.38
40	8.80	10.57	40	33.31	151.41	40	48.04	181.84
50	11.00	13.21	50	41.63	189.27	50	60.05	227.30
60	13.20	15.85	60	49.96	227.12	60	72.06	272.76
70	15.40	18.49	70	58.29	264.97	70	84.07	318.22
80	17.60	21.14	80	66.61	302.82	80	96.08	363.68
90	19.80	23.78	90	74.94	340.68	90	108.09	409.14
100	22.00	26.42	100	83.27	378.54	100	120.09	454.60
200	44.00	52.84						
300	66.00	79.26						
400	88.00	105.68						
500	110.00	132.10						
600	132.00	158.52						
700	154.00	184.94						
800	176.00	211.36						
900	198.00	237.78						
1000	220.00	264.20						

Conversion Factors:

Imperial Gallons to Litres x 4.54596
Litres to Imperial Gallons x 0.219975
U.S. Gallons to Litres x 3.78541
Litres to U.S. Gallons x 0.264179
Imperial Gallons to U.S. Gallons x 1.20095
U.S. Gallons to Imperial Gallons x 0.832674

C172 - Index

A

B

C

D

E